Working against Odds

WORKING AGAINST ODDS
Stories of Disabled Women's Work Lives

MARY GRIMLEY MASON

with a foreword by
ROSEMARIE GARLAND-THOMSON

NORTHEASTERN UNIVERSITY PRESS   BOSTON

Northeastern University Press

Library of Congress Cataloging-in-Publication Data

Mason, Mary Grimley.
    Working against odds : stories of disabled women's work lives /
  Mary Grimley Mason ; with a foreword by Rosemarie Garland-
  Thomson.
        p. cm.
    Includes bibliographical references (p.   ).
    ISBN 1–55553–630–1 (pbk. : alk. paper) —
    ISBN 1–55553–631–x (cloth : alk. paper)
    1. Women with disabilities—United States—Psychology. 2. Women
  with disabilities—United States—Social conditions. 3. Discrimination
  against people with disabilities—United States. 4. Women with
  disabilities—Employment—United States. I. Title.
    HV3021.W66M37   2004   #NUG: 6
    331.4—dc22   2004013133

Designed by Lou Robinson

Composed in Janson by Coghill Composition Company in Richmond, Virginia. Printed and bound by Maple Press in York, Pennsylvania. The paper is Maple Tradebook, an acid-free sheet.

MANUFACTURED IN THE UNITED STATES OF AMERICA
08 07 06 05 04   5 4 3 2 1

To all of the women who so generously shared their stories with me

CONTENTS

FOREWORD

Rosemarie Garland-Thomson

Mary Grimley Mason's *Working against Odds: Stories of Disabled Women's Work Lives* is much more than simply an ethnographic study of disabled women's relationships with work. This remarkable book creates a vibrant community and opens it to members who may have been loath to join what they considered a discredited lot. It invites those who are isolated by the shame often evoked in anyone who seems desperate enough to claim disability identity. To read this book is to enter a circle of women—including most prominently Mary Mason herself—whose aggregate humanity, tenacity, complexity, and plain interestingness dispel the discomfort and distance we have learned to feel about disability. The author clearly meets the challenge Simi Linton lays out in *Claiming Disability: Knowledge and Identity*: to construct a cultural narrative that is "an account of a world negotiated from the vantage point of the atypical." Mason deftly moves her readers—as she says of her subjects—"from denial to integration" about the experience of disability.

Mason crafts her community of women adroitly. Through her book, which comprises the work stories of eighteen women, Mason makes these women the active agents of their own lives. No mere case studies, their own words express their unique perspectives, even in the table of contents, which identifies every woman with a succinct quote. "Find your own life work," Alicia advises. "I don't have to make an apology," Louisa concludes. "You are put into this box," Helen observes. These women display ownership of their lives with strong, active verbs like *work, integrate, claim, redefine, struggle, reinvent, confront, cope, adapt,* and *raise consciousness.* No mere recipients of social services, these women do not wait passively for the generosity of others. Sometimes plucky and spirited, sometimes ambivalent or enervated, sometimes furious or sanguine, these fully realized human beings tell us their stories as they understand them. While their narratives compel, they do not move into the perilous space of disability inspiration. Mason presents these women in ways that refuse to imbue readers with a smug and self-centered response.

By interweaving her own story with the stories of the women she brings to us, Mason eschews the sympathy narrative and creates a cohesive community. The women come into being in relation to Mason and she in relation to them. The authorial self and the observed other emerge together through the narrative. The notion of unfolding in tandem with others is a feminist psychological paradigm that contrasts sharply with the pattern of autonomous development characteristic of the masculine individualism dominating American society today. While these women are solidly self-determined, they understand and acknowledge that interdependence, rather than independence, is the pattern of development in which their lives are most fully realized. Disability seems to help them to know this. Family, social services, and personal care attendants make possible who they have become and make impossible the isolating fantasy of autonomy that pervades our modern moment.

The most effective community-building strategy Mason employs in *Working against Odds* is also the most subtle. It is what I call the politics of pronouns. The ways discussions about disability wield the dichotomies of "we/they" and "us/them" both reflect and affect the way we collectively imagine disability and the lives of people with disabilities. The reigning convention is to draw a firm border between a nondisabled "we" and a disabled "they" that objectifies and isolates people with disabilities, shunting "them" off into a place where "we" refuse to go. This is the space where "they" become mere lessons for "us." The simple but profound "us" Mason uses is a stunning political and narrative strategy. By placing herself in the authoritative center of a community of disabled women of which she herself is a part, Mason offers a compelling perspective to govern the reader's viewpoint. By aligning her authorial perspective with that of her subjects, Mason breaks up the isolation that relegates people with disabilities to the edges of humanity as a collection of the disavowed "them." This politics of pronouns makes *Working against Odds* a gift to disabled women and a gesture to draw nondisabled readers into a community that may be entered without trepidation or scorn. The circle of "we" that Mason founds here potentially enfolds all humanity.

ACKNOWLEDGMENTS

M y interest and involvement in the disability movement and in starting this project of interviewing other disabled women owes much to my friend and colleague, Karen Schneiderman, who introduced me to my first activist meeting at the Disabled People's Liberation Front. I am very grateful for her encouragement and advice throughout the many phases of this work.

Many other people have helped me along the way, both in the conception and the writing of this project. Gail Pool helped me articulate my goals. My colleagues at the Wellesley Center for Research on Women, especially Ruth Harriet Jacobs, Sandra Jones, and Sumru Erkut, listened to and encouraged the first stages of my research. My writing group at Brandeis Women's Studies Research Center—Nancer Ballard, Paula Doress-Worters, Barbara Greenberg, Mei Mei Akwai Ellerman, Margaret Morganroth Gullette, Lois Isenman, Rosie Rosenzweig, Mary H. Terrell, and Marcie Tyre—gave generous and valuable feedback to my work in progress. In addition, my thanks to Sarah Winston, Kim Cristal, and Irene Lehrer, students in the Student Scholar Partnership program of the Brandeis Women's Studies Research Center, for their excellent assistance.

A Tides Foundation grant helped fund the transcription of the interviews, and Janna Jacobs and the Project on Women and Disability gave their backing and encouragement. Special thanks to Rosemarie Garland-Thomson for her support, and thanks to my editors, Elizabeth Swayze, who began to guide me through publication, and Sarah Rowley, who continued through to the end.

Above all, I wish to thank all the women who generously shared their stories with me and made this book possible.

Working against Odds

INTRODUCTION

When I finished writing my memoir, *Life Prints*, and reflected on my story about growing up with my disability from polio at the age of four, I realized that my knowledge of other disabled women was practically limited to the life of Helen Keller. I also recognized that I was part of a larger community of disabled people, a community I had not been eager to join. I wondered about the lives of other disabled women. Who were the others, like myself, and how had they managed, I wanted to know. How had they made it? Or had they?

Retirement from many years of teaching in a Catholic women's college in Boston freed me to start researching the lives of disabled women to find out whether they were employed and, if so, whether they were satisfied in their work and personal lives. I had been very fortunate in receiving a good education and had been employed for over twenty-five years doing work that I loved. I had married and had a family, though later I had divorced. Looking back, I realized I had struggled with barriers of gender and disability discrimination and had not easily integrated my disability into my identity. Despite my discovery of the women's movement in the seventies, I had rarely met other disabled women either in the academic world or outside of it. I decided to start a project of interviews with other disabled women to hear and record their stories.

First I needed to become acquainted with the profile of disabled women in America, particularly related to their work experience. The statistics are not cheerful: 73.9 percent of women with work disability status are unemployed, compared with 24.7 percent of women without work disability status.[1] This percentage is only slightly more than that of disabled men, but women are more likely to work part-time and earn less than disabled men.[2] The median monthly income of disabled women is 13 percent less than that of nondisabled women.[3] Disabled women's jobs cluster around service occupations and unskilled labor rather than managerial or professional work.[4] They have fewer high school degrees and fewer college degrees than able-bodied women, and their vocational training and counseling is often gender stereotyped.[5] I also discovered that disabled women are "less likely than non-disabled women to be married, more likely to marry later, and more likely to be divorced."[6]

Throughout the project I immersed myself in disability literature and scholarship. I attended and participated in conferences on disability and joined listservs and other groups concerned with disability. I have learned much, but nothing has been more valuable than the narratives I recorded in my interviews with thirty disabled women. I chose to emphasize their work experience not only because it has not been sufficiently emphasized in other studies, but also because in American society our identity and self-worth are profoundly connected to the moral imperative of work. As Rosemarie Garland-Thomson writes, "Nowhere is the disabled figure more troubling to American ideology than in relation to the concept of work."[7]

Since I was interested in finding out about the successes as well as the failures disabled women experience in the world, I interviewed women who had some work experience, although it was often part-time work and sometimes interrupted. I contacted these women through referrals, through independent living centers, or through various newsletters of organizations for the disabled. Most of them were eager to tell their stories, and many of them got in touch with me when they heard about my request for participants. Some, however, who were unemployed, felt too uncomfortable with their status to be interviewed. I have not used the real names of the women in the narratives unless otherwise requested.

The women in this group have diverse backgrounds in race, ethnicity, and class, and their ages range from twenty-seven to sixty-seven. Their disabilities are limited to physical and sensory impairments, although I interviewed a few women who also had psychiatric disorders. Their physical disabilities are diverse, including cerebral palsy, spina bifida, multiple sclerosis, and brain or spinal injuries, among others. Those with sensory disabilities include the hearing impaired and the visually impaired.

All of these women have high school degrees and most of them, regardless of their class, have had some higher education. They are, therefore, more advantaged than many disabled women. However, although they had access to education—sometimes state subsidized for disabled people—they often found it difficult to find appropriate employment or to arrange for transportation and other accommodations necessary to take the jobs that were available.

My interviews revealed a number of factors involved in the success of those who did find appropriate work: a positive family attitude, access to a social system of support, and an economic status that facilitated educational and other opportunities. The quality of education and counseling about career choices and opportunities were crucial. Finally, as for many disabled people, physical accessibility and accommodations in the workplace often determined the kinds of jobs available to these women.[8]

As I interviewed these women and recorded and reviewed the narratives, I discovered that despite their individuality, these women's stories revealed common themes. They were my themes, too. Their experiences helped to illuminate my own and to broaden my understanding of disability. I found that they talked not only about their work and how they struggled to become self-sufficient, but also about how they had claimed their disability and had owned it as part of their identity. This integration occurred at different times in their lives. Many of them identified turning points when their perception of their disability changed, sometimes from denial to integration.

Equally important were the women's accounts of how they had confronted their marginalization in society. Some became activists and confronted this attitude openly. Others attempted to assimilate into the able-bodied world, but often found themselves considered as outsiders. Their stories reflect the medical and social constructions of disability that have been imposed on them. Finally, all of the women talked about how their claiming of their disability and their confronting marginalization affected their work experience.

This book is divided into three parts, each focusing on one theme and the issues raised by it. In part 1, The Way We See Ourselves, the six stories about integration highlight issues of body image, identity, and dependency. In part 2, The Way the World Sees Us, the stories about marginalization focus on issues of identity, "passing," and social constructions of disability. In part 3, The Way We Work, the stories about discrimination focus on work and strategies for self-sufficiency. The six narratives in each section are representative of the whole group.

The narratives in part 1 particularly illustrate the different ways in which these women have made disability part of their identity. Learning from the disability movement, they see themselves as part of the diversity of society and not just as an example of a medical condition. They came to this redefinition by acknowledging and claiming their disabled bodies—their impairments. This process was particularly hard, since disabled women's bodies are frequently placed outside the norm, making it more difficult to claim them. Sometimes they feel barely categorized as women.[9] One woman in a wheelchair said she often felt like "a body without a head." Coming from an able-bodied woman this remark would suggest that she had been sexually objectified, but this disabled woman meant she had been neutered and seen more as a wheelchair than as a person. As Nancy Mairs writes in her memoir of living "waist high in the world" in a wheelchair, "The general assumption, even among those who might be expected to know better, is that people with disabilities are out of the sexual running."[10]

The process of integrating disability depends on many factors, but I found that the severity of the impairments and the age of the onset of the condition were most important in this group of women. If the disability began at birth or during infancy, as in my experience, it is often part of the woman's identity formation. However, many of these women described points in their lives when they redefined themselves, often to break out of a medical model imposed on them. If the disability came on gradually, from as early as adolescence and as late as mid-adulthood, the woman's experience parallels the general pattern of aging. Her impairments are progressive, and she goes through a series of reinventions of the self. Finally, if the disability was the result of a trauma—an accident or a stroke, for instance, that occurs in adult years and threatens a well-established sense of self-identity—she strives to restore that identity. In all cases, the women struggle with society's construction of "normality," which instructs them to divide the "impaired" and "bad" parts of themselves from the "good" and "normal" parts, making an integrated identity more difficult to achieve.[11]

As I listened to the stories in these women's interviews, I admired their struggles for integration, which often dealt with much more severe and limiting impairments than mine.

Having grown up with polio, I don't have many recollections of being able-bodied, except from photographs of myself before my illness, running and digging at the beach or riding a bicycle. Wearing braces, using crutches, and adapting to those circumstances became habitual. However, sometimes I had episodes of sheer frustration when constrained by new braces that didn't fit, or moments of terror at night when I was unable to get out of bed and run to my parents' bedroom. I practiced a good deal of denial and had dreams of being a dancer and floating as lightly and gracefully as a butterfly. When I studied literature in college and read Shelley's "Ode to a Skylark," I felt that I might overcome my bodily self and fly off like the bird. I was not really in touch with my body, and I found the transcendence part didn't work when I landed in a wheelchair for twelve weeks from a hairline hip fracture after a fall. I had not been in a wheelchair since I was six when my family sent me to President Franklin D. Roosevelt's Warm Springs Foundation in Georgia for polio rehabilitation. The accident in my forties, in midlife, when I was married and had three children, was a turning point for me, the beginning of my first real acknowledgment of my disability and of the acceptance of my body as it was.

Closely related to the claiming of a disability is the coming to terms with dependencies and the need, which varies enormously, for having care givers. Some women I interviewed are totally dependent on personal care assistants to carry out the functions of their daily lives. Others, like myself, lived for years with very little assistance, insisting on doing what the able-bodied did and refusing to take advantage of even the limited provisions society provides.

All of the women I interviewed expressed a fierce desire for independence and self-sufficiency, but each one had to accept some dependency. A delicate balance between the desire for independence and the need for assistance is hard to achieve. In Nancy Mairs's discussion in her memoir of her struggle to find this balance and not lose her own sense of "tendering care" as her MS (multiple sclerosis) progresses, she concludes, "Permitting myself to be taken care of is in fact, one of the ways I can take care of others."[12]

Some of the women found that their relationship to a care giver, often a parent, was difficult. Some had to overcome undue pressure from parents to be "normal." One woman had to fight her parents' opposition to her using a wheelchair, even though it provided her with greater freedom and mobility. They felt she was "giving up."

I experienced similar pressure from my father. Although devoted to my welfare, he would not or could not accept that I could not be cured. He took me to many doctors and looked into any new treatment that offered hope of returning my paralyzed legs to normal. His schemes seemed more oppressive as I matured, and at the time of his death from a heart attack when I was thirteen, we tragically were at odds with each other, making my grieving even more difficult.

My mother, on the other hand, was close to the ideal care giver. Always available but unobtrusive, she drove me to physical therapy sessions and swimming lessons and friends' houses and college. Even after I got a car, she helped me set up dormitory rooms and apartments. Later, she came to help after the birth of each of my three children and toted her grandchildren around during our summer visits. Looking back, I know there was tension. How do you repay someone to whom you feel so indebted? I know that I felt ambivalent about my bond of dependency. However, as she grew older, living into her late nineties, I found that my visits to her retirement home and the little attentions I could give her meant a great deal to both of us. I sensed a balancing out in our relationship.

Many of the women I interviewed discussed their relationship with a partner or a spouse after they developed a disability or a worsening physical condition. Some partnerships survived and others, like my own marriage, did not. Of the fifteen marriages (one person married three times and another married twice), seven ended in divorce. In five of the divorces, the women said their disability was a major cause. Four of the women who stayed married had partners who were also disabled. Three of the unmarried women claimed their partners left after they became disabled, and one said her serious relationship was increasingly strained. All of the single women brought up the issue of care giving and were concerned about how their disability would affect their chance of marrying or of having an intimate partner. Several were concerned about their ability to have children. These concerns about intimacy, marriage, parenting, and caretaking are well founded. Asch and Fine write, "Disabled women are commonly considered unfit as sexual partners and mothers." These findings, they explain, are based on cultural attitudes that are more negative toward disabled women than toward disabled men.[13]

There are other kinds of dependencies. Some women spoke of gradually adapting to the special needs of their disability. One visually impaired woman learned to use a guide dog and mastered Braille; another chose not to use a dog and manages with a cane. One of the hearing impaired women used a signer in our interview. Another, though fluent in sign language, reads lips and speaks, having been trained in oralism when that was mandated in the forties and fifties in schools for the deaf. All of the women who used wheelchairs believed that self-sufficiency could be improved if society provided more accommodations.

Part 2 focuses on cultural and societal reactions to our disabilities and how we deal with them. Even if we learn to accept our disabilities as a difference that changes but does not limit our identities, we are inevitably shaped by the subtle and complex attitude of the outside world toward us. Women and especially disabled women are especially vulnerable to society's stereotyping and stigmatizing. Rosemarie Garland-Thomson writes, "Western thought has long conflated femaleness and disability, understanding both as defective departures from a valued standard."[14] Some disabled women internalize these negative messages.[15] The women I interviewed were remarkably free of this kind of low self-esteem.

The stories in part 2 describe the social discrimination and marginalization these disabled women have experienced. Some have confronted this double oppression actively, becoming involved in the disability movement through protest and advocacy. Others describe the experience of trying to integrate or "pass" in the able-bodied world at periods in their life when they were less severely impaired. One woman with an invisible disability felt that it was a matter of survival in her job to hide her disability; many similarly disabled people have attested to that necessity.[16] Even those with obvious visible disabilities occasionally experienced a kind of mental passing, as in my case, where we forget that we are not part of the able-bodied world until suddenly confronted with our difference. As Carol Gill writes, "Although it may seem that only those with hidden disabilities can play the game of 'passing,' all people with disabilities are socially pressured to cover their differences and emphasize their normality."[17] In *Stigma*, Irving Goffman goes even further, suggesting that given the relative meaning of "normal," passing "is a problem that wide ranges of persons face at one time or other."[18]

The stories of the six women in part 2 describe an acute awareness of living simultaneously in two worlds, often feeling that the able-bodied world sees them as "the other." One woman, who experiences this "otherness" from both race and disability, adamantly claimed that disability discrimination was the worst.

Although I have a visible physical disability, I often mentally inhabited the world of the able-bodied, at least temporarily. However, that world could dissolve abruptly, leaving me in a kind of no-man's-land. For instance, one summer, at nineteen, when I was singing in the chorus at Tanglewood in the Berkshires, I was confronted in the dormitory by my assigned roommate, a young woman who, as far as I could tell, was mildly disabled. She walked with a limp but was far more mobile than I. As I entered our room, she took one look at me and fled. I experienced a sharp jolt of pain from her reaction to me. I felt shame and exclusion. The situation was soon remedied when I was given another roommate, a dancer, who became a kind of soul mate when we discovered we both felt like outsiders, though for very different reasons. Looking back on the incident, I realize my assigned roommate was a victim of the pressure to "pass" in "normal" society. My visible impairment was a threat to her status. I recalled that I, too, had occasionally played that part if thrown with someone more severely disabled.

Finally, part 3 brings together six stories about ways in which disabled women have coped with social barriers and discrimination in the workplace in order to find some self-sufficiency. Our work culture, so focused on productivity and fitness, is a tremendous challenge to the self-esteem and identity of disabled women. The majority of women I interviewed insisted that they experienced more discrimination from their disability than from their gender, but they also identified times when they felt double discrimination.

The six women in part 3, who were able to own their disability and feel good about themselves, represent different ways of confronting the difficult task of finding meaningful work. Their narratives illustrate patterns representative of the whole group.

Of the thirty women I interviewed, fourteen worked or were retired from full-time employment and thirteen worked part-time. Three women were not employed. Even though all have some education beyond high school and many have graduate degrees, the majority (nineteen out of the twenty-seven women working full- or part-time) were employed in fields related to disability. Only a few, like myself, had unrelated careers, including civil engineering, history, nutrition research, biochemistry research, and a flower business. As studies have shown, women as a group find themselves employed more in service occupations and other areas traditionally considered "women's work," but disabled women are even less likely to make it into professions or management positions and are further ghettoized in disability services.[19] They are more likely than able-bodied women to work part-time and to have periods of unemployment.[20] In the six stories in this last part, two women work full-time, one does not work, two work part-time, and one is a student. Three of them receive disability insurance.

All six women described some kind of disability discrimination in their work experiences. It ranged from the refusal of prospective employers to give interviews to denial of accommodations after employment to negative stereotyping on the job or in job placement. The women's stories show different ways of confronting these barriers: they include open confrontation—filing a lawsuit or complaint, for instance—more passively adapting or attempting to assimilate, deciding to leave the traditional job market, and finally, choosing not to work at all.

The lives of all of the women in this study are, like mine, intertwined with disability history in America. I identified closely with five of the women who were born in the thirties and grew up, as I did, in the forties and fifties. While at that time many other disabled people were still institutionalized, their welfare considered a matter for charities, these women, like myself, were educated in the professions. Our impairments were not severely limiting when we first entered the job market in the late fifties or early sixties, and we had opportunities in fields open to women, such as teaching and counseling. Two women, breaking out of the traditional mold, pursued careers in science. There was very little public consciousness then about disability rights even though we had a president, Franklin D. Roosevelt, who was a polio survivor. Without policies or legal guidelines to follow, we had to act as if we were not disabled or at least as if our disability would not hinder us in any way. At interviews for jobs, the subject of our disability was avoided. I remember feeling uncomfortable in an interview about ignoring the fact that I used crutches. Neither the employer nor I mentioned it. Afterward, I wondered if I should have assured him that I could carry out all that was expected of me. I still wonder if that lack of communication was responsible for the jobs I didn't get.

Another common experience I shared with these older women was more discrimination from gender than from disability. At least we thought so, although I now suspect we were ignoring the way the able-bodied world saw us. I became keenly aware of the old boy network in graduate school at Harvard and how it cultivated the young men for the preferred academic positions and left the women to fend for themselves. But I was reluctant to recognize that my disability might have saved me as an undergraduate from the open sexual harassment that some of my Radcliffe classmates encountered from male professors. Now I wonder if I had simply been ignored as a woman because of my disability, despite my academic honors.

Women born in the forties and fifties make up the largest group in this study, and among them are some pioneer activists who, in the late sixties, fought disability discrimination and, in one case, even helped to shape public policy against it. Those entering the workforce in the late seventies and in the eighties, after the passage of the 1973 Rehabilitation Act, were certainly aware of the emerging disability movement. In the seventies, individual disability groups realized that united political action could create a social and political force and began to lobby for disability rights.[21] The provisions of the 1973 act laid the groundwork for legislation against discrimination in employment. In the 1980s the Independent Living Movement started with the goal of deinstitutionalizing the disabled and helping them become mainstreamed in society.[22] And in 1990, the Americans with Disabilities Act prohibited discrimination on the basis of disability. Because of these national developments, the younger women, born in the sixties and seventies, went into the job market with higher expectations, even if they had limiting impairments or were in wheelchairs. Some did benefit from the changing climate. Others found their expectations have not been met, but they are less willing to compromise.

My experience of interviewing and listening to the stories of these women and my knowledge of disability literature and scholarship have shaped my approach to this material and to many issues in disability discourse. I have made a conscious decision not to editorialize the narratives but to let the women's voices, which express a variety of opinions, be heard. I give their stories a context both in relation to my own experience and as examples of disability issues. Jenny Morris, in *Encounters with Strangers* and in her other writings, has warned us not to ignore the actual experience of disabled women and their impairments in our legitimate fight to oppose the social and economic oppression disabled women face.[23] In an essay in *Hypatia: A Journal of Feminist Philosophy*, she writes, "The problem is that if we don't express the experience of our bodies, others will do it for us."[24] And she argues that we need to put back the experience of impairment into our politics.

In these narratives I have tried to convey the actual experience of these women. Disability has profoundly shaped their lives and identity, as it has mine. These women's stories describe their struggles, strategies, and triumphs.

1 The Way We See Ourselves

In *Recovering Bodies*, Thomas G. Couser argues that disability narratives that treat the body as a central component of identity—like gender and race—have added something new to life writing. He says, "Life writing about illness and disability promises to illuminate the relations among body, mind and soul. Disability narratives," he contends, "may further illuminate the ways in which the body mediates identity and personality."[1]

The narratives I have collected, though not written by the persons themselves, are still an oral form of personal narrative and not only tell us much about the life experiences of disabled women, but also convey something of the individual's sense of selfhood. The six stories in part 1 particularly focus on how these women came to perceive and claim their bodies, with their impairments, as an integral part of their identity, giving them a stronger sense of who they are.

This process of integration does not always come about easily, and it is difficult for both men and women. In writing about four types of integration in disability development, Carol Gill notes that "people with disabilities have had to separate and individuate from a parent culture that fears and devalues disability."[2] Society still separates, stereotypes, and stigmatizes the disabled and particularly disabled women, who experience the double bind of belonging neither to the dominant male culture nor to the subordinate culture of able-bodied women.

These stories describe the process of how the women interact with their disability, and although each story is unique, they show some similar patterns depending on when the disability occurred. Debbie and Elaine, born with their disabilities, share stories of how they struggle to get other people—their families or doctors, for instance—to accept them, with their bodies' limitations, as they are. They want help to function better in their daily lives rather than pressure to work for some miracle cure. Debbie, born with cerebral palsy, describes several turning points in her life when she made decisions that gave her more authority over her body and more freedom to become herself. Elaine's story traces her journey from a dependent, institutionalized young African-American to a mature adult who found work that she enjoys despite her serious condition of osteogenesis imperfecta, which fosters bone fractures.

Virginia and Doris, whose disabilities came on gradually and progressively, tell of how they redefine themselves as disability becomes a greater part of their lives and redirects their relationships, ambitions, and careers. Virginia, once a person with 20/20 vision became totally blind in her twenties. She compares the stages of accepting her loss with Elizabeth Kübler-Ross's description of the mourning process in *On Death and Dying*. Doris has one of the nine types of muscular dystrophy, resulting over many years in a deterioration of muscular control. She sees her life as a series of stages of overcoming her denial of her disability and of gradually being able to integrate it into a fuller sense of identity.

Alice and Louisa both became disabled from sudden and unexpected trauma. In midlife Louisa had an aneurysm and blood clot, resulting in some memory loss. Alice suffered a spinal cord injury when, at twenty-one, she accidentally fell from her third story apartment when she was washing windows. Although the stories of these two women differ significantly in the nature of their impairments and in the timing of the traumas, they both had to come to terms with claiming their changed capacities. In her narrative, Louisa relates how she was determined to return to being the able-bodied and successful lawyer, wife, and mother she had been before her trauma. She discovered that she had to acknowledge that her identity now included her disability, but that she could still maintain her professional and personal self. Alice, an active young woman who was a horse trainer before her accident, had to adjust to a totally different body and changed expectations. She says, "I have come a long way. I am so proud of myself."

In their narratives these women also acknowledge that the process of claiming their disability was not up to them alone, since "disability is not simply located in the bodies of individuals."[3] It is also "a product of cultural rules about what bodies should be or do."[4] Society's idealization of the healthy, independent body imposes an impossible standard on the disabled and devalues their vulnerability and need for some dependence.

The question of how much importance to place on independence is a feminist issue. Feminists have questioned a value system that distrusts and devalues dependence on other people and vulnerability in general. In *Feminism and Disability*, Barbara Hillyer discusses the care giver and the disabled: "Disabled people force us to face the problem of reciprocity."[5]

In their stories of seeking self-sufficiency, these six women tell of their coming to terms with dependency. Whether it was accepting personal care assistants or wheelchairs or other special aids, they learned that these accommodations not only were necessary but also made them freer and more self-sufficient. They also tell us about "interdependence," or as Hillyer calls it, "an acknowledgment of the way lives intertwine."[6] In fact, these women discovered that the knowledge and limitations they have experienced can be valuable not only to them but also to the able-bodied world. As Carol Gill writes, "Disabled people are proclaiming their distinct value because of disabilities."[7] Doris finds that she is a better psychotherapist because she knows "what it feels like to be broken," as one of her clients told her. One of Debbie's strengths as a social worker is her skill in mediating between doctors and patients in the veterans hospital where she works. Louisa has learned to rethink the way she relates to many people, both in her family and at work, and Alice feels she is more sensitive to other people's needs since her accident. Both Elaine and Virginia have made it their vocation or career to educate the able-bodied, particularly in hospitals, schools, and other institutions, thus breaking down the false boundaries that divide the two worlds.

These six storytellers speak from their lives as women: three are married, two have children, three are single. All of them are employed or have been employed either full- or part-time. The work they do bolsters their self-image and helps to validate the self.

DEBBIE

"My disability is not who I am. It's something I happen to have."

interviewed Debbie in her sunny one bedroom apartment on one of the upper floors of a subsidized apartment building that gives her a view of the city. Born in 1950 with cerebral palsy, she is a social worker at a veterans hospital and works an average of four days a week. She uses a wheelchair and hasn't walked for the last fifteen years or more. Two cats appeared from time to time as we talked, and one in particular gave Debbie affectionate rubs before stalking off. Her speech was difficult to decipher at first, but I soon caught on to the rhythm of it and understood her very well, including her witty commentary.

In discussing her family, Debbie said that her father, though always able and willing to finance her needs and education, had a hard time accepting her disability. Her mother also found it difficult. As Debbie's main care giver, she became so identified with her role that she saw her daughter's failure to improve her walking or to "get well" as an indictment of herself. Debbie recalls the day she was nosing around in the cellar and found some old medical records that described the difficulty her mother had in coming to terms with Debbie's disability. The conflict of her mother's attitude and Debbie's reaction to it framed Debbie's home life until she left for graduate school. She says, "She would always push me to do everything I could do, which was good, but she would never accept [my saying], 'I'm tired. I don't want to do that today.' She never knew when to stop." Debbie adds, "I wonder sometimes what my life would have been like if she was still alive."

Her mother died of cancer in 1984, Debbie's first year in graduate school.

Debbie's primary and secondary education was in special schools for the disabled, which, she says, were not very good, particularly in preparation for college. Her high school class was the first one to have any students going to college, so the school had not developed a college preparatory curriculum. She was given speech therapy, occupational therapy, and other programs for her disability but very little academic training. She graduated in 1970 at the age of twenty.

Her college experience was not much better. Her first year at a college in New Jersey near home was, she says, "a big mistake." She arrived on the campus three years before section 504 of the Rehabilitation Act of 1973 outlawed discrimination against "otherwise qualified" individuals in federally funded programs and thus began pressuring colleges and other institutions to accommodate disabled students. Debbie was not given any special assistance. She summarizes her feelings about her first year in a college community: "If someone from Mars landed, I'd know exactly how they felt. I lasted a year." The next year she attended night classes at another university, but this time her mother accompanied her to classes and took notes. Debbie began to wonder why she was struggling to go to college. She knew her parents expected her to get a degree, but as she says, "They never asked me if I wanted to go." She decided to take a couple of years off, a decision that was the beginning of her attempt to claim her own life. After several years, however, she felt that she wanted to finish her degree and found a state college that offered courses by telephone. In 1982, twelve years after she started college, she graduated with a B.A. in psychology.

Debbie's life was turned around in 1984 when she visited a friend in Boston who helped her set up an appointment with the dean of students and dean of admissions at a graduate school of social work. "I basically talked my way in," she says, and she found the school a very positive and supportive place. They had a disability office that worked together with the school to get her what she needed, including work-study students to do her writing. "They did everything they could," she says, "and particularly the dean of students was always in my corner. She parted the waters more times than Moses." With financial help from the state rehabilitation agency, she was eventually able to complete a graduate degree in social work.

Another major turning point in Debbie's life followed the year she turned thirty-four. She decided to get a motorized wheelchair at the suggestion of her friend, a physical therapist, who urged her to make the transition from the extreme limitations she had in walking to the greater mobility a wheelchair could give her. Debbie remembers her previous confinement: "I could get around the house, but I couldn't go outside. I couldn't go downtown and I couldn't go to my own doctors' appointments." All that changed when she bought the chair. But her family's reaction was negative. Debbie exclaims, "Oh, my God! When I got this chair, they had a heart attack! [They] saw it as giving in."

But when she told her friend about her family's attitude, her friend reassured her. She said to Debbie, "Ask yourself, if you didn't have the chair, could you walk down Commonwealth Avenue with me?"

"No."

"Could you go to grad school?"

"No."

"Then I guess your family is just going to have to live with the chair, aren't they?"

Debbie summed up the event. "When I got my first motorized chair, it was like I'd been let out of jail." Her family did eventually become supportive and pleased with her new freedom.

Her new freedom helped her to decide to leave home and break her dependence on her mother, so she set herself up in an apartment with the aid of personal care assistants and began to thrive. She recalls another turning point in her life sometime after her mother's death. It was another moment when she acknowledged that accepting the limitations of her body was liberating and not defeating. At the time, she was seeing a therapist regularly. She usually consulted with the therapist by phone, but every few months they met for dinner because, as she says, "We needed some eye-to-eye, one-on-one contact." At this particular time, after they had met in a restaurant and had been served, Debbie started to laboriously feed herself, a task very difficult for her spastic hands to accomplish. She describes the scene:

My therapist, Sandy, said, "Debbie, we can do this the hard way or the easy way. You can feed yourself and we won't get to talk, *or* you can let me feed you and we'll get to talk and have some fun."

And I remember saying to her, "My mother would have a fit."

And Sandy stood up—we were at a table in a corner—she stood up and looked around the restaurant, then sat down and said, "Debbie, I don't see your mother here."

I've never forgotten that. And she was right. She wasn't there. And Sandy's point was, it's your life, not your mother's.

Debbie has fifty-eight hours a week of personal care assistants (PCAs). They are financed by Medicaid, but she finds and hires her own PCAs. They come and get her up in the morning—the time varies depending on her schedule—and return to give her lunch at her apartment or at work. About 4:00 P.M. they run errands for her and give her dinner, and later they help her to bed. As Debbie says, "My life runs around their work. But they're all very good and they're all very reliable. If it weren't for them, I couldn't live independently." She adds that she is not always lucky in finding good assistants and knows that the scarcity of reliable personal care assistants can be a major problem for many disabled people.

When she finished her master's degree in 1988, Debbie thought she would like to work with young people, but she had an interview with the director of a state-run facility for veterans. The director was so enthusiastic about Debbie taking the job that she talked her into it and became a friend and mentor. Debbie works with patients who are mostly elderly veterans who live in the facility's dormitory, and she confers with their families, particularly the families of the patients on the Alzheimer's ward in the hospital section of the facility.

At first the nurses were skeptical of her, she says, but recently one of them remarked, "You know, we were really mean to you," and when Debbie replied, "Yeah, you were. What was your problem?" the nurse said, "Well, I think some of it was your disability and some of it was that we didn't want a new social worker. But every day you kept coming in and coming in, and pretty soon it was like we couldn't ignore you anymore."

In fact, the staff got so used to her that when she got a new wheelchair, they didn't even notice the change. They couldn't believe it when she told them she'd had it for three or four months. "They didn't notice it," Debbie says, summing up her colleagues' attitude toward her disability. "It's not what they look at, which is what I'm trying to say. You make your disability a big deal, they're going to, too." She concludes, "My disability is not who I am. It's something I happen to have."

When I asked if she found it difficult to work on the Alzheimer's unit, she says, "Mostly, yes. You watch the patient going downhill right before your eyes, and you have families that have to make some very hard decisions and some decisions you know they are going to regret."

Debbie finds her role is often to interpret what the doctors tell (or don't tell) the families. She's critical of doctors' failure to explain the consequences of their medical orders. For instance, she says, a doctor suggested to the family of one of her patients that a feeding tube be put in to help him swallow and told them it could be taken out at a later time. But Debbie intervened.

"I said, 'Wait a minute, hold the phone here. Right now, you're not taking anything away from him. He's not eating, but that's his choice. Once you put in the feeding tube, you're not going to take it out because that means he's not going to get food.'" The family decided not to put in the feeding tube.

"They're idiots, the doctors," she concludes.

When asked if she ever considered changing jobs, Debbie admits she has thought of it. But as she explains, "A few years ago I really wanted to leave. But when I started looking around, it dawned on me that I didn't want to start all over again and have to convince people all over again that I could do the job."

"They know I can do the job," she says of her fellow workers, and she has found a cooperative environment. Lately, she has had increasing problems with disks in her upper and lower spinal column, and has had to have surgery, but she still continues to work. She concludes, "I think having been able to keep my job, keep going at my job, is a testament to me but also to the place I work."

Debbie thinks that more disabled people could work if they really wanted to, but she admits that not enough is done to show disabled people how they can work, keep medical benefits, and organize their lives. "It's only in the last fifteen or twenty years that disabled people have been out working and out in the world and not sitting at home."

As for herself, she admits that her family's pressure and support did give her the impetus to be an active member of society. In addition, she had some good advice from friends and some good luck. But equally important is her ability to claim her disability and contain it.

Deborah Jackson died on November 20, 2002. It is believed she had a stroke, not necessarily connected with her disability. This telling of her story is dedicated to her memory and is in her honor.

In April 2003, I contacted Debbie's brother, David, for permission to publish her story as she told it to me. We had several phone conversations and e-mails, and he agreed to write a brief commentary on her narrative and on his and the family's relationship to Debbie and her disability. I found his reaction to Debbie's story an example of the sometimes painful complexity of the dynamics in a family with a severely disabled member. He revealed issues of acceptance, of dependency and independence:

> I'm pleased that [Debbie] will be included in your book because her accomplishments will be an inspiration to others who are disabled. I loved my sister very much and was very proud of her. I knew Debbie one way. I never treated her differently because of her CP. She was just my sister. What was lacking in her physical abilities was balanced by her brilliant mind.

In our conversations David conveyed a sense of shock to find that in her story Debbie expressed anger at her mother and a desperate need to extract herself from her family in order to empower herself. He felt that Debbie had not understood how much her mother had done for her:

> Debbie was the product of a young couple who, at age twenty-two and twenty, "happened to have" a handicapped daughter. Her drive and ambition to find her independence was fueled by the dedication and pledge that my parents made to Debbie that she would live a fulfilling and accomplished life. Debbie was a

brilliant soul, and my parents were very proud of her and always believed in her.

My mother made a vow to herself that Debbie would surpass every discouraging word passed along from doctors who said that she'd never speak, walk, or attend school. Does a parent ever accept a child's disability? Maybe acceptance means giving in to the disability. By giving in, would Debbie have succeeded so?

About his own and his family's relationship to Debbie, David wrote:

Having a handicapped sister forced me and my siblings to grow up quickly. I feel like we were adults by the age of six. I would fix Debbie's lunch, vacuum the house, and do laundry to help my exhausted mother who worked full-time and had four children to raise.

Since Debbie's death, I've spent a lot of time thinking of our past together—our family, the tough times and the good. I wonder if other families with disabled children share the sadness, envy, resentment, coupled with joyous holidays, happy birthdays, celebrated births, and incredible accomplishments my family dealt with through the years.

Disabilities force those affected to be more resourceful and to find alternative ways to make life work. It's not only the disabled who are affected, but the family who loves them as well.

And finally, after I had commented in one of our conversations that I believed Debbie appreciated her family but that claiming her independence was her strategy for survival and self-sufficiency, he wrote:

Debbie's tough exterior was really her defense mechanism, I guess. I never really thought of the psychological implications of Debbie's disability because she always seemed so strong, sure, and accepting of her situation. Thank you for your insight. You put things into a different perspective for me.

David concluded that Debbie's narrative should be published just as it was.

ELAINE

"We've lived with this disability all our lives; we know what our bodies feel."

When I arrived at Elaine's one bedroom apartment in Boston, I saw what seemed to be dozens of stuffed animals perched around the living room walls, chairs, and windows. Elaine laughed. "My children," she said, as I looked over the menagerie. She was so tiny that she—a smiling, energetic African-American woman—was almost completely contained in the seat of her wheelchair.

In our interview Elaine conveyed a level of comfort with herself and her body. She was born in 1957 with osteogenesis imperfecta, which had impaired her growth and subjects her to bone fractures. She attributes her attitude toward her disability partly to the fact that she was born with it and partly to the hospital schools for the disabled that she attended. Since her parents' house was not wheelchair accessible—they lived on the second and third floors of a triple-decker—she stayed much of her youth in institutions, coming home for holidays and for some weekends. She didn't find it a negative experience. She says, "For me, that's all I really knew. And I made a lot of friends there."[8] At twelve, she went to another hospital school where she boarded most of the time until she graduated from high school. She describes the school as helping her develop physical independence and confidence in advocating for herself. The staff, she says, was very practical and matter-of-fact about the students' disabilities. Their attitude was "OK, you're disabled. This is how you're going to live with it." The other advantage of the school, she notes, was that she met other disabled children. "[They had] different disabilities," she adds, "but I was able to learn from them and they were able to learn from me." At seventeen she developed a hearing impairment, and she now wears a hearing aid and has learned sign language. Elaine experienced the community of disabled students as a positive influence in her perception of her disability.

On the other hand, she feels that the school was not academically strong and did not prepare her for college-level work. In a way, their positive acceptance of the students' disabilities was a disincentive to helping them shape a future and a career. "The goals I had as a kid were unrealistic," she says, "like I wanted to be a nurse, a pediatrician. And the nurses would just say 'Yeah, yeah,' humoring [me], though it was obvious these were goals [I] could not achieve." As she got nearer to graduation, she began to think about other possibilities and to set more realistic goals, including working with children or becoming a receptionist, which she is now doing in a hospital.

Elaine feels that one of the most significant consequences of her experience with institutions was losing touch with her family and her place in a working-class black culture. She says, "Basically I grew up in a white culture. Whereas my parents are black. My two brothers are black. They grew up in a black culture." She realizes her experience has separated her from them. She concludes, "Although I always felt that I was black, to be honest, culturally, I'm more white. And I think that's hard on my family."

Despite the separation, her parents have been loving and protective even though they had very little support from the medical world or from social services. In the sixties and seventies, programs for families with disabled children were very few, and no one in her family was sophisticated in the ways of managing the medical establishment. She feels that her mother felt a lot of guilt. "She never talked about my birth. I don't think she totally understood about the disability," she says, adding, "She doesn't like to talk about me being disabled and still sometimes calls me her little girl. I think she thought I'd always be home and needing to be cared for!" About her father, she says, "He's very stoic. He's in total denial. Again, he never talked about it [the disability]. He worked a lot so he was hardly home. And I think a lot of times he compensated by giving me a lot of material things. That was his way of dealing with it."

Although her high school education did not meet very high academic standards, it did integrate work experience into the curriculum. By her senior year she had a job three days a week as a mail clerk in the city, and she was transported to her job regularly. When she graduated in 1978 at twenty-one, she was offered a full-time position, but she didn't want to continue that kind of tedious work. She began volunteering in a day care center and found that she loved helping children.

The year 1979 was a turning point for Elaine because at twenty-two she left home to live independently and began to work part-time at a children's museum. It was a big transition in her life, she says, because for the first time she had to keep to a schedule, get a calendar and an alarm clock, and plan her time. She says, "[It was] real scary. I had to get used to it. I had to train myself to know when it was time to eat, that you eat three meals a day. I had to train myself to think that way."[9] She also remembers the joy she felt when she first experienced the freedom of going to the movies or shopping when and where she chose.

Elaine's self-sufficiency is supported with some outside help. She lives in an accessible and subsidized building and uses The Ride (a public transit system for the disabled) for transportation, though it is notoriously inadequate. She also has some home care aid through social security disability insurance (SSDI) for cleaning and laundry and occasional food preparation, but she has learned to do everything else for herself. Like many other disabled people, Elaine's life redefines the concept of independence. She is dependent on some personal care assistants, but they enable her to maintain her independence and live a productive life.

Elaine stayed at the children's museum for four years and simultaneously started community college courses in child development, which she found very helpful in her work. At this point, her goal was to be a teacher's assistant working with young children. Earlier, she thought she might adopt a child after a doctor told her that childbearing would be impossible because of her size and condition. Although she ultimately decided that physically and financially, adoption would be too difficult for her, she knew that she liked to work with children. She says, "I [knew I couldn't] have a child of my own, so I thought, 'OK, what am I going to do to fulfill those needs?' I [decided] I would be a teacher's assistant."

She was hired at a preschool for children ages three to five who are behaviorally or cognitively disordered. "It was exciting," she says. "It was really a good experience. I worked with a wonderful teacher and we learned a lot from each other."

Elaine feels she gained a new awareness of the world in that job. She discovered a harshness from which she had been sheltered. The children, she says, had often been abused and to her "it was like an eye-opener. Reality." She often wondered, "My God, do people really do those things to children?"

One of the rewards of the work was that she discovered she could help children "so that they were not hurting themselves or someone else." Although some of them were very aggressive and she was vulnerable to physical attacks, she found that they rarely tried to strike out at her. She recalls, "They might have hit my wheelchair, but I only had one kid who hit me. He hit me in the face, but he wasn't very strong anyway."

Somehow, she says, despite their own rage and disorder, they accepted the fact that she was fragile and had to be treated carefully. And yet they also respected her as one of the staff. She stayed there five years, working three days a week with a very supportive group of people. However, she admits that "it was a very draining experience."

After another year and a half in a similar program for children—though a less well-organized one—Elaine began to think of a job change. She heard of a position as a receptionist in a hospital, and this turned out to be another turning point for her. She felt the job would combine her interest in people and their needs with her interest in advocacy, which she had been doing along with her other work. She says of the job, which she now has, "I'm actually killing two birds with one stone because I'm indirectly doing disability stuff. People come to me. They see that a disabled person can work. Children can ask me any questions. So I'm doing two things at once!"

Elaine had to file a discrimination complaint with the Massachusetts Commission against Discrimination (MCAD) to get the job. This was an important experience for her because she learned what her rights were and how to fight for them. "I was quite proud of myself," she says. The hospital, which ironically has a training program for disabled people going back to work, clearly did not want to hire her. First, after she applied for the position, they told her they had lost her résumé and application. Then when she supplied another one and checked on her progress, she was given conflicting information about an interview and actually never met anyone in the personnel department. In fact, her only interview occurred after hearing she did not get the job. She insisted on being told why she was not hired. In this meeting Elaine realized she was practically given (unwittingly by the interviewer) all the material she needed for a discrimination suit. She recalls that first, the woman said Elaine didn't have enough experience with money (the job had very little responsibility for financial transactions) and then that she didn't come from "a Harvard teaching hospital background" (clearly irrelevant for a receptionist). But finally the woman concluded with a third reason that Elaine describes gleefully as "the killer":

"This person said to me (and they were remodeling the hospital's lobby), 'Well we're trying now, with the new lobby, to present a certain image.'" Elaine adds, "And I thought to myself—Lady, you just killed yourself."

She promptly filed a discrimination complaint and a month later, she was hired. She's been there for several years, likes the job, and feels no hostility toward the hospital or it toward her. The experience gave her better insight into the discrimination that the disabled community experiences, and it gave her more confidence in her own ability to deal with the world of employment.

Elaine's interest in teaching and her ability to connect with people have given her a vocation of advocacy for the disabled. She has been advocating since she graduated from high school, but it is now an important part of her life. She gives talks at elementary, middle, and high schools, at businesses, and to medical students, particularly second-year medical students. But she starts her consciousness raising in her own workplace—in the hospital where she works. First, she has to teach her colleagues that every disabled person they see is not necessarily a patient. She has often been mistaken for a patient instead of an employee. Then she has to help her coworkers understand when to offer her assistance. She tells them not to assume she is unable to do something, but rather ask her what accommodations she needs to make things easier.

But it is with the students—in schools or at the medical school—that Elaine feels she can make the most difference in educating people about how to relate to the disabled community and how to see them as ordinary people who happen to have a specific difference. She has been going to one middle school in the suburbs for ten years. They asked her to come originally because they had a disabled child in the school and wanted to help the students and teachers relate. Since then they've asked her to return every year. She says that for sixth graders, she concentrates on talking to them about attitudes toward the disabled and draws them into discussions with questions such as "Do you think it's easier or harder for a person to be born with a disability or develop a disability later?" When President Clinton was in a wheelchair briefly, she brought up another question: "If the president is hurt and in a wheelchair, would you consider him a disabled person?" After a few questions like that, she has them involved.

"I'm able to get the kids to talk, to really talk," she says. "It takes a while. The first five minutes it's a little sticky, but once they realize I'm not there to judge them and that this is their opinion, it becomes a good discussion."

She often finds that her discussions don't just stay in the school. She has had parents say, "Oh, you talked to my kids at school. They talked about you." In this way, she is able to get her message to adults, too. With really young children, preschool and kindergarten, she becomes part of their play in the classroom. She'll paint with them or join their games. Then she'll let them sit in her wheelchair or push it around so that they begin to get some understanding of her disability and how it is part of her life. Outside of the classroom, when she meets children, she tries to make them feel at ease because, as she says, they don't necessarily know what a wheelchair is and might even find it frightening. With adults, however, she says, "I feel they need to work it out. I don't have to put them at ease; they have to do that on their own!"

Elaine's favorite challenge, however, is the medical school students. She goes to the school at least once a year. "I just love going there," she says. She talks about her typical visit:

I go with one of the orthopedists I know. When he first asked me to go, I said, "I'll come with you, but there's a deal here. You can talk as much as you want about medical stuff. I don't care. I'm already a medical textbook for these people. But when it comes my turn to talk, I'm not going to focus on the physical me. I'm going to talk about behavior and attitudes, of how doctors need to work with disabled people and I don't mean in the physical sense.

First she emphasizes the need to really listen to a patient "in terms of [her] body." As she says, "We've lived with this disability all our lives; we know what our bodies feel." She gives an example from her own experience when she went into an emergency room with a broken bone in her leg. "I've broken bones all my life," she says, "and I know that when a person has OI [osteogenesis imperfecta] the break does not always show up on the X ray." But the doctor would not believe her and insisted on taking an X ray, only to discover that nothing showed up.

She also warns students of the danger of assuming that children who frequently come in with broken bones are automatically considered to have been abused by parents. They need to be checked for OI, she cautions, so that families are not wrongly accused.

Another point she tries to make is the importance of seeing the person as an individual and not just as a person with a disability: "You can get ten people in the room with the same disability, and we're not all alike. There are different needs, different personalities." She insists, "You need to look at your clients." Remembering her own childhood, she says, "Nothing is more infuriating for a child than to have a doctor or therapist talk to her parents as if she doesn't exist, as though she was not part of the treatment."

Finally, she tries to get the medical students to see disability outside of the medical definition, which thinks of it only as something to be cured. "I have to get them out of the mentality of being the caretakers," she says. "I always say, 'Look, you're not going to cure us. So don't try! Make us function.'" For example, she tells doctors that they have to give up the idea of having her walk. She says, "Look, I know you are into getting people to walk [but] I'm more dependent on my

wheelchair, so just knock off with the walking! Get me functional!"
Coming back to her main point, she says, "We're going to know what's
best for us."

Elaine finds that many of the medical students do listen to her.
Sometimes, she says, she'll run into them later and "they say they
learned something," which gives her great satisfaction. She has also
given time to public organizations, committees, and businesses, but she
particularly likes the direct contact with different kinds of students.

I asked Elaine if looking ahead, she thought she might be doing
something different. She answered wryly, "You mean if The Ride
doesn't kill me first?" And then she mused, "I don't know. I might be
back in the classroom, but it's a lot of work when you have those little
ones in your care. And the other factor is my disability. So I don't
know. I can't think that far ahead."

VIRGINIA

*"[It was] my first inkling of what
it was like to have a difference."*

interviewed Virginia, who is totally blind, in a small local library. Walking with her guide dog, this young-looking woman
arrived soon after I came in. We found a quiet corner to sit and
talk while her dog settled beside her chair. At forty-three, Virginia was
used to telling her story and had found time for our interview in her
busy travel schedule. She had just returned from San Francisco where
she had spoken at the California Academy of Sciences and was about
to leave for Montreal, Canada, to conduct workshops in diversity
awareness.

Virginia's loss of sight was completely unexpected. Growing up, she
had 20/20 vision, so when at eighteen she began to have difficulty
seeing, she thought she just needed glasses like the rest of her family.
By the time she was twenty, it was clear that she was losing her sight
due to diabetes. Like many people who experience the gradual onset
of disability, her story illustrates the stages and turning points she went
through as she coped with her changing relationships among herself,
her family, and the world.

In her first year of college, when Virginia went to an ophthalmolo-
gist to get glasses, she was immediately sent to a specialist. Thus began
a frustrating medical journey from New York to Boston, from one
doctor to another, none of whom could give her and her family any
straight answers. They could not or would not say whether the deterioration was irreversible. Meanwhile, her sight was getting so poor that

she had to leave college. She says, "I couldn't read the numbers on the door."

Finally, about a year after many appointments with specialists, her parents took her to Johns Hopkins Hospital, and there a doctor spoke to them bluntly. Virginia recalls the moment.

"He said, 'There's nothing we can do.' I remember this distinctly. My parents were sitting there. This guy did not have much bedside manner. He was talking into his tape recorder for his notes at the same time."

They were all in shock, but particularly her parents, who felt guilty because they thought they had failed to take proper care of their diabetic daughter. Virginia recalls, "At that point I felt I needed to take care of my parents a little because I think pretty much from early on— since I had watched [my sight] deteriorate—I kind of expected it." However, she says the doctor claimed he had never seen such rapid deterioration before.

"It was scary," Virginia remembers, "to try to keep up emotionally." She adds, "I was acutely depressed." She explains that she was used to dealing with depression by burying herself in a book, but now she could not read even with magnifiers. To make matters worse, none of the doctors informed her or her family about services that were available to the visually impaired. "I didn't even know they existed," she says. That changed when a friend of hers looked in the yellow pages of the phone book under "blindness" and found New York's Commission for the Blind. Soon she was able to get a tape recorder and talking books, and she began to learn Braille. Her spirits were also lifted when the director of the summer camp where she had worked for many summers insisted that she could come back. She had a great summer with young children who accepted her impairment without question.

Her family was having to adapt as well. She became close to her younger brother, who was still at home in high school. In fact, she taught him to drive, which amused them both. As he said, "It's a good thing you couldn't see me." But it took everybody a while to adjust. She has a big extended family and many friends who supported her. She remembers her grandfather, who lived down the street from them. "[He] was a wonderful man. He used to come every day to check on me. He was the quintessential Italian gardener, and he used to bring me really fragrant flowers out of his garden, which was really wonderful."

Gradually Virginia felt enough confidence to return to college, but she went to a university nearby so that she could live at home. At college she found that she had to completely readjust to the way she learned. "All of a sudden," she says, "everything was audio, not visual. I still consider myself a really visual person. I was one of those people who could look at a text and memorize it." With determined effort she learned how to transform from visual to audio skills. By the end of the year Virginia realized that not only had her learning methods changed, but she herself had also changed and she began to feel smothered living at home. So she applied to colleges in the East Coast and ended up at a small prestigious New England college. Here she was to experience another challenge to her identity.

She found that people didn't quite know what to do with her at the college campus. She lived on campus her first year as a junior and then moved off campus with some friends the next year when she decided to get a guide dog. "I wasn't a good cane traveler," she says. "Using a cane just slowed me down significantly." She got a black Labrador and went to a dog training school. Now she found herself defined as the blind girl with the dog. She was even confused with another blind female student who had graduated several years before and whose dog was a completely different breed. "All of a sudden I realized I wasn't an individual, I was a *blind*," she says, adding, "It was really my first inkling [of] what it was like to have a difference. I'd been brought up as an intelligent, middle-class, white woman and never felt there were any issues as to my ability to do whatever I wanted. And that changed."

The realization that she had limitations on what she could do panicked her. In response she decided that she would have to achieve a 4.0 grade point average that semester so that she could be accepted. As she says, "I thought then I would be like everybody else." Achieving that goal was difficult. She had no computer or voice synthesizer at that point. She had three tape recorders and a typewriter. She worked out an elaborate system. She explains, "I still wrote out my notes [from class] because I had this particular type of clipboard that had thick lines down it, and [I] could move this thing so I could write between it.

Then I would have somebody read my notes back on tape for me." If she had to write a paper, she would have two tape recorders next to the typewriter so that she could use the material as she wished.

Her professors were very supportive, particularly one professor who recognized her panic when her first paper was due. He told her to relax and "get the [paper] to me when you get it to me." After she turned it in, he pulled out a bottle of champagne to celebrate, and "we sat around [his office] and yakked," she recalls. She adds, "He was also a good friend's thesis adviser, so we would go over to his house all the time and have dinner with him and his wife."

By her senior year when Virginia lived off campus she had many good friends, some of whom remain in contact with her. She also dated, but she characterizes the dates as "guys, none of whom I liked very much." Besides her dog training school, she was also trained by a rehabilitation instructor in cooking so she could take her turn making meals in the house and be prepared to live independently when she left college. She speaks appreciatively of the rehab instructors she has had over the years. She remembers in the first years of losing her vision the importance of a mobility instructor to help her find her way around the house she had known since childhood. She recalls, "It was extremely disorienting. I'd be in my parents' living room, which is a huge open space with cathedral ceilings and stairs close at hand. And I would always be afraid of getting turned around." With instruction, she learned how to orient herself. She explains, "You hear the street, and you can hear the birds out the front windows. You can hear the refrigerator in the kitchen."

In 1981 Virginia graduated with a B.A. in psychology, abandoning her original premed major. The effort to achieve this independence and academic excellence completely exhausted her, however, so that after graduation she went home. "I basically slept for two months," she says. When she recovered her energy and realized that living at home was not a good idea, she decided to move to Boston where some of her classmates had gone and where she now shared an apartment with some friends. She would experience another shock as she tried to find a job and discovered she was again stereotyped as "a blind" and as someone incapable of work, despite having managed four years of college.

Having attended a liberal arts college, Virginia had very few practical skills and wasn't sure about what kind of work she wished to do. Many of her friends took temporary jobs in bookstores and as waitresses while they decided whether to go back to graduate school, but since she couldn't do those kinds of jobs, Virginia decided to try volunteer work to broaden her experience. She was shocked at the response. When she called potential organizations and gave her credentials, they were interested and enthusiastic, but at the end of the conversation when she said, "Oh, and by the way, I'm blind and use a guide dog," there would be a complete change. First there was silence, she recalls, and then the response would be, "Oh, I don't know if that will work here." Virginia was frustrated and angry. "I kept thinking," she says, "Oh my God, I just graduated from a college that's usually considered one of the top three in the country and I tell them I'm blind and it negates everything." She continues, "[I] left college feeling [I] could conquer the world, and all of a sudden [I] was slapped down for wanting to do some volunteer work."

Finally, although it was not what she was looking for initially, she volunteered for an organization for the blind. "They kind of curve you right into that," she said, "because no one else will hire you." Soon she became connected with an elder service agency, dealing with elders with visual problems, and this led to a paying job as a counselor and also as a trainer in a residency program for ophthalmologists. She became an advocate for the elderly and the visually impaired, giving public talks in nursing homes and other settings—all work that would help form the basis for her present business.

This public work gradually brought out a more self-confident and extroverted side of Virginia. She notes, "I'd always been very shy prior to losing my vision," but she realized even in college that unless she spoke to people first, they were going to avoid her. However, when she started going out to give presentations, her boyfriend had to drive her there and push her through the door, saying, "You will be fine." Eventually, she says, she became comfortable in front of groups of people. In fact, she adds, anybody who has met her in the last fifteen years or so can't believe she was once reserved. "You were shy?" they exclaim unbelievingly.

After working for three years, Virginia went back to college and got a master's degree in social work. Her experience there was a contrast to her undergraduate college years. No accommodations were made for her at any level—neither from the faculty nor from the college administration. When she went to the dean about access issues, including the difficulty of getting advanced course syllabi so she could order her books on tape, the dean accused her of not being able to keep up with the work. The university was so indifferent and hostile that after graduation, she considered filing a disability lawsuit but finally decided against it.

Her internship experience was better, although she found that people were nervous initially about giving her work. At her first placement at an eye and ear infirmary, she had trouble convincing her fellow workers that she was an intern and not a patient, but eventually she won the staff's confidence and had a good experience. They even hired her for replacement work the next summer. Another internship was at a mental health clinic, which she particularly enjoyed. While there, she wrote an article for a journal refuting the argument that a blind therapist cannot work with children. This article, eventually read by another visually impaired student in a social work graduate program, led to his seeking her out, getting to know her, and eventually becoming her husband.

After receiving a master's degree in social work in 1991, Virginia started another round of job interviews and found the same kind of discrimination. "At that point, I was ready to shoot people," she says. "You had to constantly explain how you were going to get to work, how you get your clothes on straight, and how you're going to get around the building." After having had enough of explaining to everyone how she functioned in everyday life, she made an important decision: "I decided I was going to have people *pay* me [to explain all that]."

She stopped looking for a job and through a friend started working in a science museum as both a volunteer consultant and a guide, explaining exhibits. Soon she was on a staff committee on access and then, supported by a grant, training staff on disability issues. "We ran six training sessions on different types of disabilities for the staff of six different museum departments." She adds, "It broadened my knowledge about other disabilities." This work expanded into other grant-supported training sessions around diversity issues. Before long she was handing out business cards to other museums, to institutions, and to corporations where she gave public talks and conducted training workshops on issues of diversity. As part of her cultural institution work, Virginia also helped to create museum exhibits based on the principle of "universal design," which argues that what works for people with disabilities also enhances the experience for other people as well. The design creates an inclusive way of providing information and uses multisensory approaches.

Virginia feels that advocacy and educational work suit her more than working as a therapist, where she found it difficult to keep her objectivity. She and her husband, who was a chef before he lost his vision, travel all over the country. "You're really working with learning styles and how to educate people best," she explains, and "I'm really comfortable doing that." She adds, "I think my way of [dealing with] being angry at other people is to do this kind of stuff. I think this is my coping mechanism."

Virginia's work, as her own life experience has taught her, is to emphasize the importance of understanding disabled people as individuals, not as statistics. "I think what happens with any group that has a difference is that people come to see them all in a clump. They don't see individuals." In her programs she insists on sensitivity training before she discusses theory or the Americans with Disabilities Act (ADA) and other legal questions. In fact, she expresses some concern about the effects of the ADA regulations. The institutions, she says, will say, "OK, I need to do X, Y, and Z, but I don't need to do anything else." In her training sessions, she focuses on the why of the ADA, not just the code itself. She says, "I don't think anybody learns anything from [the code] other than how high to make something so you can get a chair under it. But if they understand they are dealing with humans as individuals, they are more likely to make [the code] stick."

Virginia admits that at times it is wearing to have to continually educate people about disability issues. Often when she and her husband are walking with her dog and trying to discuss their work, they will get interrupted repeatedly by people who love dogs, asking them how the dog was raised and trained. Despite the inconvenience of the interruptions, she tries to be gracious. As she says, "I feel that it's imperative for me to educate people about these issues, and unless they feel relaxed, they're never going to get it."

As for her family, she says, "I knew my dad was going to be OK when he called me up one day and he told me a blind joke."

Virginia experienced panic, frustration, and anger as she went through the stages and reinventions of claiming her disability. But when she described to me the "first inkling of what it was like to have a difference," she was characterizing herself as *having* a difference as opposed to *being* different. She does not accept the world's reductive perception of her disability as her identity. Her work grows out of her personal understanding of what the able-bodied world needs to learn in order to empower the disabled community and acknowledge that disability is one of the differences, along with race, gender, ethnicity, and sexual orientation, that make up a diverse society.

DORIS

"A friend said, 'I've always been amazed that you continue to reinvent yourself.'"

oris, a sixty-four-year-old psychotherapist, has also experienced a gradual onset of disability. She has one of the nine types of muscular dystrophy, resulting over many years in a deterioration of muscular control, particularly in her feet and legs. At present she uses an electric scooter, a wheelchair, and a van.

She and I met in a restaurant for her interview. We also had an informal follow-up interview over lunch about a year later and arranged to meet in the town where she lives. Arriving a little early at the inn we had chosen, I went out on the front porch to wait for her. As I stood looking down the street, I saw a stylish older woman who nodded and talked to people as she drove briskly along the sidewalk on her scooter.

Doris traces the onset of her disease to age six when she was clearly limping. She remembers a neighbor commenting to her mother a few years later, "There's something the matter with the way that kid walks." Perhaps alerted by that remark, her family took her to doctors in New York when she was eleven. Numerous tests yielded no definite diagnosis, so her family continued to ignore her condition.

Doris remarks, "It was like no one said, 'The emperor has no clothes.'"

Years later her mother expressed regrets that they had not done more about her disability. She threw some light on their state of denial when she said, "You know, your dad couldn't handle it—that you were less than perfect." Her younger brother has never really discussed her disability, though he helps her get her wheelchair into her car when they meet. Doris summarizes her own attitude toward her disability—which probably mirrored that of her contemporaries—as she became a young adult and went to college: "The only way to fit in was just to pretend it wasn't there."

Doris describes high school as divided into parts—one good and one bad. At a Catholic high school in New Jersey, she was a "total depressed wreck," acne-prone and unhappy. She wasn't able to perform in physical education, but the school made her take it anyway. When she transferred to another high school, everything changed. "I emerged like a butterfly from a cocoon," she says. No more acne, new clothes, and a boyfriend! She could play the role of the popular fifties teenager. In her first year of college she was pushed into "secretarial sciences," as many of her female classmates were, even though she wanted to major in English. When her father was transferred to Massachusetts, she changed colleges and majored in English literature, but her family insisted that she live at home to save money. They also took in another student, who shared her room. Doris found this arrangement difficult, and she says she was eager to get engaged partly because it offered the prospect of moving to a place of her own.

Six weeks after graduation in 1958, Doris was married to a young man she met in college. She remembers having difficulty climbing the steps to the church. One of her aunts—she was later told—remarked, "How is that child ever going to be [able to be] pregnant?" But as Doris says, "I had a baby nine months and one day after [the wedding]. That's what Catholic girls did in those days. I had four babies in four and a half years." She remembers her first pregnancy as being extremely difficult. She had very little strength and could hardly get up from the couch. The other pregnancies were easier. However, the increasing strain of all of her domestic responsibilities was hard. Doris comments, "There didn't seem to be any alternative. I mean, in those days, nobody said it might be good if you spaced your children." There was no money for child care. Her husband had not finished college when they married, and he was just starting to work. Doris recalls that her mother and her husband's aunt rescued her with some help with the babies.

A friend remembers visiting Doris during this time. She was pregnant, feeding one child in a high chair, and carrying another one on her hip. Her friend recalls, "I was astounded how you [could do all] that."

It was after her fifth child that Doris, almost by accident, had her disability diagnosed. She had gone to see a doctor about a dermatology problem from relentless diaper washing for five years. When the doctor saw her walk in from the hall, he asked, "What is the matter with your legs?" and told her to sit on the examination table. She recalls the unexpected events that followed:

> So he did tap, tap, and says, "You have Charcot-Marie-Tooth [a form of muscular dystrophy]." He knew right away and said, "Here, go to the brace clinic."
>
> So I went up to the brace clinic and I was crying. I mean it was all very shocking to me.
>
> Later the doctor said, "Why are you crying? Did you like the way you walked?"
>
> He was very unfeeling. I mean he really was. And I was not a particularly feisty [person], but I said to him, "Why don't you sit up on the table and I'll tell you to put on braces and see how you feel."

Doris concludes, "And anyway so that's the brace [*pointing to her foot*] prescribed, exactly those with the black shoes and the double uprights."

When she arrived home, she found little comfort. Her husband— "God love him, a theater major," she says—made her situation *his* tragedy and soon had the children crying as he lamented, "Your mother has to have braces."

Doris sees this moment as an important turning point in her life. "The braces," she says, "in a large way were a way out for me." No longer "barefoot and pregnant" all the time, she switched to wearing slacks and vowed to learn to walk gracefully in the braces. In 1970 she went back to work, teaching Hispanic children in Head Start.

"It was a whole new revelation for me. It was wonderful!" She studied Spanish and spent two weeks for two summers in Puerto Rico living with a family to perfect her language skills. Her husband was at first supportive in staying with the children, but finally he left them in April of 1973. The marriage had been in trouble for several years, exacerbated by a mutual drinking problem.

As a single parent of five little children, Doris, still working, managed to start a graduate program part-time in religious education and theology in June 1973. One of the most important means of survival and recovery for Doris was to further pursue her intellectual interests, pushing herself to another level of learning and "spiritual transformation."

"I've always wanted more, to learn more, to do more," she comments.

Besides her intense interest in theology, particularly female spirituality, she discovered the women's movement—somewhat clandestinely—in the seventies. She describes herself "with five little kids reading [Germaine Greer's] *The Female Eunuch*!"

Another major turning point in Doris's life occurred in 1975. That year she got divorced and also attended her first Alcoholics Anonymous meeting, challenging another aspect of denial in her life—alcoholism. She reflects, "I know that the drinking was part of the whole denial and escape, and I'm very grateful that very early I got the wake-up call when I was still young." She has celebrated her twenty-five-year anniversary as an AA member.

Doris's master's degree in religious education got her a job in counseling substance abusers and coordinating a hospital program for alcoholism. She also taught in a certification program at a community college. Although she enjoyed her work, she realized that she liked doing therapy, so once again she set out to redefine herself. In 1987 she started another graduate program and in 1990 received an M.S.W. (Master of Social Work) that would enable her to practice as a therapist. As one of her friends has said to her, "I've always been amazed that you continue to reinvent yourself."

Meanwhile, Doris had remarried in 1984, this time to a fellow member of AA and a teacher. They moved to Florida in 1990 where Doris worked for five years as a therapist in a family services program. Before she left for Florida and while working and studying, she also pursued new developments in her medical condition. She had a battery of tests for muscular dystrophy, which included what she believes was an unnecessary nerve biopsy in her leg—done probably for medical research purposes—which resulted in damage to her ankle and leg. The swelling that now occurs regularly requires that she wear compression stockings. Only recently has she finally found responsive and responsible medical help. She visits a neurologist who has given her a thorough reevaluation and prescribed a helpful rehabilitation program that includes learning to drive a van with a lift to give her mobility. She has insurance from her ex-husband's health plan and also some state medical insurance.

The move to Florida with her second husband resulted in a particularly significant crisis in Doris's life. Working full-time, she found that her physical condition was deteriorating. She was using a wheelchair and realized that she needed more assistance in getting around. Her husband was not able to handle her changing needs. She recalls the climax of their relationship:

> He said, "I'm not a caretaker. I don't want to be a caretaker."
>
> It was one of those revelations when I was crying and he was yelling and I just said, "I'm just trying to survive here." And he replied, "Go do it somewhere else."

Although his response was brutally honest and cruel, Doris remembers that after the initial shock she said to herself, "That's a good idea! Why didn't I think of that!" She knew that he would not leave. He had said, "I'll never leave. I won't leave." She recalls saying to herself, "I can't think of anything worse than being progressively disabled and being dependent on somebody who feels like that." She remembers, "I took my car, my chair with the motor, and my clothes, and I left."

Doris now had to acknowledge the progressive nature of her disability, but she resolved to make herself as independent and self-sufficient as possible. She returned to Massachusetts, to her father's house on Cape Cod (her mother was no longer living), and found work as a therapist.

Soon after, she decided to return to Florida where she rented her own apartment and had a practice for three years. Then she began to think of another vocation that had attracted her for some time, a vocation consistent with her intellectual and spiritual development. She decided to enter a monastery run by Benedictine nuns, a place she had visited for a good part of a year while she was in Florida.

Her plan was ambitious, but she persuaded the nuns to take her on as a late vocation, and she moved to the monastery in Florida in 1998. She recalls her stay there fondly. Warmly received, she found many friends and intended to continue working, as many of the members did, to help support the community. However, six weeks after her arrival, she developed pneumonia, and after her recovery she ruptured her biceps tendon trying to maneuver her wheelchair around inaccessible buildings. Living in the monastery was too physically taxing. Furthermore, Doris adds, "It also became very clear to me that I was going to be terribly lonesome for my children and grandchildren. I'm a very social person, and I felt very isolated and very lonely." When her daughter said, "Come home," she decided to return to Massachusetts to live closer to her and to pursue her work as a therapist.

The monastery experience, however, was important for Doris as part of her own spiritual journey in which she continues to ponder the question of suffering: "I think a lot of my connection to spirituality, frankly, has been trying to explain disability to myself. And what I have come to on my good days is, [I] don't understand but I trust!"

Although she has no theological answers to the question of suffering, Doris, a "recovering Catholic," in her words, had her own personal vision and illumination, which she recounts:

> One morning I was just feeling so discouraged. I was having trouble getting out of bed, and I looked at the cross and I had never seen this before, but I saw on the cross the immobility, not the pain, but, you know, the immobility.
>
> And I thought, on the cross, Jesus was a quadriplegic.

She went on to reflect on her spiritual revelation: "I think there is a way you can use spirituality to bolster denial, but I also think there's a connection with something deep within yourself that is very healthy."

Doris recalls the stage in her life when she discovered the literature on disability. She recalls that just as she read Gloria Steinem and Germaine Greer surreptitiously in the 1970s, she started to read books on disability in the 1980s, such as Irving Goffman's *Stigma*, in the same way—"like one of those [books] you have to spirit into your pocket and take into the bathroom to read."

At that stage she felt the need to hide her disability. She says, "It became a little secret that I couldn't tell anybody because, first of all, they'd be embarrassed and secondly, they would be afraid, and they'd think it was going to happen to them. Thirdly, they would feel sorry for me. My daughter calls it [hiding my disability] 'doing a Doris.' She teases me [about still doing it]."

Doris's perception of the outside world's view of the disabled is insightful. Her mention of embarrassment and fear defines people's need to distance themselves from the disabled as the "other" in order to assert their own superiority. Her rejection of their sympathy—"they would feel sorry"—suggests her own refusal to be reduced to a victim or martyr.

Now in her sixties, Doris feels comfortable with recognizing her disability. Her grandchildren even tease her gently, giving her gifts that she can't easily drop—knowing her hands have become weaker. She admits that at times she still does not identify herself as disabled. Recently, she was asked to be on the Jerry Lewis telethon for muscular dystrophy, and after her appearance, she watched the video of the show, which included a shot of her getting into her van from her wheelchair. She was amazed to see the difficulty she had in maneuvering, particularly the trouble she had using her hands.

She also recalls that she once had a hard time accepting the idea of using a wheelchair. She says, "Having to be in a wheelchair [was] the nightmare of my life." But she adds, "Now it seems to me like an avenue to freedom again." Furthermore, she says, "I have a relationship with a lovely man who's in a wheelchair." He wasn't disabled all his life. According to him, he told his son that if [he] ever goes out with another woman she is 'going to have to be in a wheelchair or she is going to have to rent one.'" Recently, Doris and this gentleman were married.

Doris concludes with a credo that her life story illustrates: "I'm not willing to be trapped in this body." At first her independence was based on denial, but her intellectual and spiritual development helped her to claim her disability as part of herself as a woman with talents and capabilities. Like many who grew up before the disability movement gave the disabled community encouragement to expect accommodations from society, she created her own solutions and made adjustments herself. Now as her impairments increase, she is learning—with the help of good rehabilitation advice—to keep her freedom by mastering the use of hand controls on her van and by adapting to an electric wheelchair. She lives in a subsidized accessible apartment and uses home health aides when necessary.

Doris finds that her disability has helped her as a therapist. Many people are referred to her because of chronic illness or other types of disability. She recalls that one of her patients said, "You know why I wanted you to be my therapist? Because you know what it feels like to be broken." Doris adds, "Who needs a Teflon-coated therapist who doesn't understand any of the difficulties?"

About her own positive attitude toward her life and her disability, she says, "I think having a good attitude is sort of a double-edged sword because it can be used for a lot of denial, or it can be used to say, 'You know it happened, you can't deny that it happened, but you deal with it.'"

LOUISA

"I don't have to make an apology."

I met and interviewed Louisa, an attractive dark-haired lawyer, in her office. She had heard of my request for participants and contacted me to say she was willing to be interviewed, though she wished anonymity. At forty-one, she suffered an aneurysm and a blood clot, resulting in some memory loss. Despite this trauma, she is confident and very articulate. She greeted me cordially and wasted no time in starting the interview and telling me her story about her determination to regain her old identity as wife, mother, and lawyer.

She gave a clear account of her life and career before her injury and then a detailed account of her medical experience, followed by a description of her drive to return to work six months after her hospitalization. As she says, "I was just so determined." Throughout the interview Louisa spoke forcefully and concisely, but she was disturbed if she could not find a word or a name immediately.

She often compared the "old Louisa" with the "new Louisa." For instance, when she is describing her efforts to learn new terminology in a new job, she says, "Louisa actually had to practice that word. The old Louisa would have picked it up after hearing it two or three times. The new Louisa heard it and read it twenty or thirty times. Had to make it an objective."

At one point, she hesitated on a word and said, "See? I just made a word mistake. OK?" And she continued, "And now I am tired because we've been talking and I've had to concentrate hard. So now I have to find my word."

When I suggested, somewhat frivolously, that I find that as I get older, I quite frequently lose a word or don't remember a name, she brushed aside my comment. Later she admitted that being the kind of person she is—quick and self-confident—it is harder for her to accept her present limitations. She says, "I never really had to cope with that [forgetting things or searching for words]. That's a big change."

Louisa was the oldest girl of ten children in her family. She explains her role in the family:

My mother relied on me. My mother is a wonderful, loving mother of her ten children, but she needed help. She became overwhelmed when I was a little kid. When she was twenty-five years old, she had seven children. So by the time I was six years old, I carried one of the twins; my brother carried the other twin. I was a baby-sitter, I was a cook helper, I was a housekeeping helper, I was everything. I had very heavy responsibilities. So I was a very feisty person and I would give them back a lot of mouth and I had quite rebellious teenage years. It was remarkable that I got my act together and went to college.

Louisa did go to college and graduated summa cum laude in 1975. She married and had her first child, a girl, at twenty-five and worked for the Department of Welfare, counseling women how to get out of welfare and go to school so they could find profitable work. One of her clients, she says, was interested in going to law school, so Louisa investigated what it takes and how to get financial aid. "I determined that it was really a very doable thing if you wanted to work hard enough. So I went to law school!"

She graduated from law school in 1985, and after passing the bar exam she took a position at a hospital as its labor and employment attorney. Her son was born in 1992.

Looking back, she realizes she began to have severe headaches in the fall of 1994, but she didn't take them seriously, not even mentioning them to her doctor on October 11 when she saw him about bronchitis. Then on October 13, while she was at home on a sick day with her two-year-old son, her aneurysm burst on the left side of her brain. She describes the scene:

I do not recall this at all, but I did manage to pick up the phone and somehow got connected to the ambulance. I was just crying and I couldn't tell them where I lived, so they traced the call. My daughter, who was fifteen at the time, happened to come home on an early dismissal day from school and found in our front yard two police cars, an ambulance, a fire truck, and her mother lying on the living room floor, half naked, blood coming out of her ear.

Although luckily Louisa was transported by helicopter to a major hospital and had surgery to tie off the artery, her actual brain damage was the result of a blood clot that occurred two days later. She says, "The brain damage from the ruptured aneurysm would have been extremely minimal. But the clot did destroy. And the portion of the brain where the clot was is memory, so that's why my disability is in that area."

In just six months Louisa went back to work part-time, and within the year she had returned to full-time work. She found her employer very supportive and accommodating about her recovery, but unfortunately in 1996, it merged with another hospital and her position was eliminated. She was back in the job market and still struggling with adjusting to her disabilities and to her new sense of what she could do. She notes, "My husband says that my self-confidence deteriorated badly when I had the brain damage. I know it did. As I said, I was a very feisty person before this happened."

Her determination to continue her professional career prevailed. She recalls, "I was told at the time I was discharged from the hospital that about 50 percent of the people who had my kind of medical experiences would be able to work, but not necessarily in a professional capacity. But I knew I could continue to work [professionally]. The odds were against me, but I wouldn't give it up."

Louisa took a new position working as a labor attorney in the local government of a neighboring state. Since she could not drive safely and commute, she took an apartment, leaving her husband with the children during the week. She had decided not to tell her employer about her disability. Although the ADA's protections against discrimination do not differentiate between persons with visible or invisible disabilities, many people with hidden disabilities choose not to disclose their limitations in interviews, fearing they will not be hired. Louisa decided not to disclose her medical past, and so the pressure on her was even greater because she knew she could not ask for accommodations and had to give the extra effort demanded in a probationary position. She explains:

> Now I'm in a new environment, on a new job. What do you have to do? You have to impress. It's a probationary period. They're thinking, "She did great on the interview; her résumé looked good. But is she as good as she seemed?"

The commute, the long days, and the pressure all drained her stamina, so perhaps it is fortunate that the job did not last. It had been created by a county commissioner who went out of office. Once again, Louisa had to face the job market. "I was very depressed for a couple of months," she says. Her unemployment benefits were running out, and she and her husband had promised they would find money to send their daughter, who was graduating from high school, to college. "So it was either get a decent-paying job or make a major change financially."

At present Louisa works full-time as an attorney in a government agency. She did not tell them of her injury when she was hired, but has since told her boss and some other colleagues. She has had to make adjustments, but she has an important position of responsibility and is appreciated for her expertise.

Reflecting on the particular issues of invisible disabilities, she says, "I think—and I hope this doesn't sound self-centered—some disabilities are easier for people to understand than others. I know some have been easier for me to understand. Invisible ones—especially brain injuries—are tough for somebody in a leadership role."

One of the conflicts she discussed is whether she should ask for assistance—a secretary, for example—because of her disability or because she just needs help—to do her job well. She put it this way: "Do I say to them—and I still have this dilemma—do I say to them, 'I need a secretary because I have a disability'? or do I say to them, 'I need a secretary because as far as I know, any other employer with this number of employees has a secretary'? What way do I put it?" She did finally get a secretary, and as she says, "That makes a heck of a difference." She is now able to focus on the things she wants to accomplish.

Louisa's husband, a lumber inspector at a sawmill, has been very supportive throughout her trauma and readjustment to work. Her children have, too, but it was particularly hard for her daughter, a teenager when the injury occurred. She explains, "We were always very close. When I had my aneurysm, [my family] did not expect me to live for three weeks. They were so upset that they probably didn't explain to this fifteen-year-old girl what they should have. And she didn't hear what she didn't want to hear. So when I did come home from the hospital, she rejected me. I wanted to return to being her mother. She did not want to return to dependency, because you know, you could lose your mother just like that."

Despite this, Louisa feels that the trauma was a kind of growth experience for her and her daughter. She concludes, "It interfered with our relationship about as minimally as any [other experiences between] mother and teenager." However, she adds, "My fifteen-year-old daughter wanted her mother to be 100 percent recovered. My daughter's now twenty-one and she still wants me to be 100 percent recovered!"

Her son was not quite two when she was hospitalized. "He doesn't remember the incident," she says, and "he's grown up with a mom that has a little bit of a memory problem. So he's taken it as part of his life." If he occasionally reminds his mother that he has already told her something, his father firmly explains that she has come home tired after working hard all day and needs to be accommodated.

Louisa's schedule has been very demanding. She is away from home from 7:00 A.M. to 7 P.M. "Day care opens at 7 A.M., train leaves at 7:30. It takes exactly thirty minutes to drive from my house, drop [my son] off at day care, get to the train, and park. I put on my makeup on the train because I have no time to do that in the morning. And I've tried to work on the train rather than rest, which was a mistake. I haven't accepted—I still struggle with—the fact that sometimes the best thing I can do for my employer is to rest. And one of the things that makes that difficult is that other people don't understand."

Louisa admits that she still needs to gain confidence, but she is beginning to realize that her personality has made it harder for her to accept her disability. When I pointed out to her that even people without brain injuries have problems with memory, she agreed, "It's helpful for me to hear that." She continues, "I have a disability and I also have a personality, and I don't have to make an apology."

How much of your old self can you regain? That is the dilemma for Louisa, who seems to be resolving it, but not without a struggle. Regarding her job, she emphasizes the necessity for her to maintain a different standard of energy and work from other employees: "Am I allowed to have a busy weekend and come in tired on Monday? Other people do. Are they as tired as me? Probably not. So because of my disability, am I supposed to do less of a personal nature? I *have* to do less of a personal nature. Of course I have to do less. But should I do *even less* so that I can come in sharper on Monday morning? For a long time, I was doing much less, *much* less."

Louisa continues, "I recently have decided that I'm entitled to some happiness, too." She and her husband have bought a used mobile home in New Hampshire next door to her mother. Now the family can get away occasionally for a weekend. She concludes, "I'm entitled, every once in a while, to come in exceptionally tired on Monday because I spent time with my family. I'm entitled to do that and I don't need to feel apologetic."

ALICE

"I have come a long way. I am so proud of myself."

Alice explained to me that when I came to her house, I could park in the driveway and get into a small electric lift—like a cable car—that would take me up to her second floor back porch. That was exactly what happened. Alice was looking for me when I arrived, and she instructed me how to get into the lift and how to operate it.

Alice is in a wheelchair, having received a spinal injury at twenty when she accidentally fell while washing a third story window in her apartment. A self-confident young woman looking even younger than her thirty years, she greets me warmly and directs me to her kitchen, where we sit at a table as she offers me refreshments. As the interview begins, she describes her accident and the difficult process of adjusting to and accepting a new kind of body, as well as rethinking all of the expectations she had for her life.

Alice describes what happened when she lost her balance and fell out the window ten years before:

> Your first instinct is to put your arms out when you fall. I landed on my hands and my legs flipped over me. They went backwards. I shattered both wrists, and I had multiple fractures up and down my spine. Since the break through my back was just below the chest, I lost voluntary movement from just below chest level.

She was in the hospital one and a half months, where she had surgery to put rods in her upper back for stability and an external fixator—"like a big outside Erector set"—on her right arm because of the severity of the break in her wrists. She also had a cast on her left arm.

Alice describes her four months in a rehabilitation hospital as one of the most difficult times of her recovery. As she was taken off some of the heavy medication, she realized what had happened to her. "I was devastated," she says, "very, very devastated. Very depressed. Prior to my accident, I worked with horses. I had been riding horses since I was five years old. They were my life."

She realized not only that her career was gone—she was licensed as a trainer to teach English and Western riding—but also that she had to "fight," as she says, to adjust to her new self and her different body. She explains, "The fight to be able to dress myself and find out that I have to use a catheter and a bowel program. It's very degrading and it's embarrassing."

Alice has high praise for the rehabilitation facility. The therapists, she says, were very good, and despite her slow start because she couldn't use her hands, she learned how to take care of herself. "Now," she adds, "I'm totally independent. I don't need any assistance at all."

However, Alice recalls that it took about three years to overcome her depression and refocus her life after she left rehab and came back to live in her mother's house. She gives credit to the National Spinal Cord Injury Association (NSCIA) and other organizations, such as Northeast Passage, for helping her find her way. She says of the NSCIA, "It's a group of people who are disabled in some way, and they just welcome you with open arms. It gives [you] quite a bit of confidence." Her family members, too, have been supportive. "Oh, if it wasn't for my family," she says, "I wouldn't be where I am today. Really. My mother, my brother, and two sisters. It's just my mother and my brother who live here now. And we're all very close. My two sisters and I talk to each other every single day. My brother and I are extremely close." Her relationship with her family has not always been good. She explains, "I had it pretty tough when I was younger. I was the black sheep of the family, and I had a tough life. I lived on my own since I was seventeen. I was a very wild adolescent, I would say. I quit school."

As one of the youngest women I interviewed, Alice reflected many issues relevant to young disabled women, including her relationship with men. A major blow to her after her injury was that her fiancé left her. They had been together for five years, and she had experienced a miscarriage before the accident. After her return from rehab, she explains, "the visits were less and less, and then he said, 'I just want to live a normal life.' That's what he said to me, and then he walked away."

Alice does not hide her anger: "I think he was a coward. After what we had gone through in our relationship, including the miscarriage. We were extremely close, so it devastated me. I think he saw the chair and not me. You know? He didn't see me as Alice anymore; he just saw a wheelchair. And I think it was embarrassing to him, to go out with friends and have somebody [with him] in a wheelchair who can no longer dance or who has a hard time playing pool."

I asked Alice if she had found any difference between the way men and women dealt with their spinal cord injuries. She had some reflections on her experience:

> I think when a man becomes paralyzed it drastically cuts down his self-esteem. It takes away his confidence, especially in a relationship. Especially with a nonparalyzed woman, [whom] he can no longer scoop up. It's his masculinity. As for a female—it's depressing. Your confidence goes down, but I think you have an easier time in a relationship.

Alice explained that she thinks the traditional female role of being taken care of may make a relationship easier for a disabled woman, but she also had some observations about able-bodied men:

> They're very cautious. I have had able-bodied males approach me. I am very confident when I come into a place. But it's harder to keep a relationship, I have found, with a man who is not disabled in any way. They just don't understand. They don't grasp it. What concept is it they don't grasp? I'm not sure. I got much more out of the three-year relationship with a gentleman with transverse myelitis than with an able-bodied man.

I asked Alice if she wanted to have a family. She replies:

Do I want a family? Yes, I would love to have a family. But now I have this endometriosis [diagnosed about two years ago] hanging over me. They might have to do a hysterectomy to cure it, if that's the problem. My mother asks me, "Are you ready for that [the operation]?" And my response is that if it's going to make me calm, with no spasticity [she has been experiencing severe spasticity recently], no stress—if it's that or [the chance] to have children, then no, I wouldn't want to [have children]. Because what kind of life can I give a child if I'm going to suffer like that? And there's so many children out there who could be adopted. So that's what I think is the turnaround.

Alice reflects, "I have come a long way. I picked myself up when I was devastated and could no longer have my horses. My fiancé left me. I lost my apartment. I had to find a new way to support myself. It was very hard."

After the accident, Alice enrolled in an adult diploma program and got her high school diploma in 1993. She got further training in Microsoft Office and as a PC specialist, taking courses funded by the state rehab program. She talks about the jobs she has had and how difficult it was to get started. She says, "I wanted to get off social security [disability]. I had nothing. You were looking at a country girl who used to just walk around in work boots and deal with horses."

Thanks to the state rehab agency, she acquired computer skills and landed a job at Bank Boston where she worked for two years as a Boston-Plus specialist and as a supervisor dealing with high-end customer telephone calls. She also worked in an import-export company when she moved to Colorado for about nine months. She was in a relationship with a man who has transverse myelitis and who was skiing for the U.S. Disabled Ski Team. Since he had to leave her in the wintertime to ski, one year he said, "Why don't you come along?"

"And I did," Alice says. She continues, "What a beautiful place! I don't like snow, Mary, and it could snow four feet in one night. But let me tell you, my heart will always be in Colorado!"

Her job was in town and her condo very close by. She says, "I would literally go out my back door, and just push [my wheelchair] two seconds, and there's my work, there's a post office, bank, and shopping center!"

When I asked Alice if she was interested in riding a horse again, she replies, "No, and I'll tell you why. I was very good at what I did, and I could ride any horse with any amount of spunk. I think it would devastate me to have to get on a horse that is very sluggish. A horse with high spirit could be very dangerous to somebody like me who is paralyzed."

Alice seems to have transferred her energy and enthusiasm for riding into several sports—skydiving, waterskiing and snow skiing. She explains that she sky-dives in tandem—strapped to her instructor, who pushes them out of the plane. Later on that afternoon, she showed me a video of her skydiving. It was breathtaking.

The video started by showing her in the plane, her parachute and her instructor strapped to her. She was smiling and eager as they hurled out the door of the plane into space. Then they were in free fall for what seemed to me much too long a time, falling through the sky, the plane no longer in sight. And then the parachute opened and they floated through the air, down and down, the only object in the sky, and finally landed on the earth—a good landing, she was told by everyone waiting at the bottom to congratulate her.

Alice also speaks of scuba diving—her "newfound fantasy," she calls it. She has also done waterskiing—with one ski. She sits in a little cage with her legs strapped to the board. She has taught disabled children how to water-ski in a program at Northeast Passage. She comments, "Mary, let me tell you, the smile on [the children's] faces was just fabulous! It paid for it!"

She has also enjoyed traveling—to the Florida Keys and to New Orleans. She drove to New Orleans for Mardi Gras in her sporty little black car, which I had noticed in the garage. She travels mostly by air, however, and often used to take her beloved shepherd-husky dog, Jake, whom she had for thirteen years.

"He used to run with the horses," she says, "and in Colorado, he would run with the prairie dogs. When I worked, he used to go right under my desk and stay there. He was my best friend. He could never be in a room I was not."

Alice recalls taking Jake on the plane back and forth to Colorado. The first time, when they came home for Christmas, she put him in an animal crate and he barked and howled the whole way. The next time Delta Airlines gave her three seats and he sat beside her. She says, "Isn't that amazing? I had never heard of that. He sat up on the chair and he looked behind him, looked out of the window, wagging his tail, like he knew where he was going."

It was very difficult when Alice had to put Jake down last year after all their years together, but she says, "I knew that he had a fantastic life." She's been calling breeders and is going to see some puppies soon. "I need to get another one," she says.

"I guess I have a gift with animals and children," she continues. "Is it their attention span I can grab? Or is it my personality? I can't give enough to animals and children, can't give enough."

Her physical recovery has not always gone smoothly. In the last two years she has had increasing problems of spasticity in her legs. She was put on so much medication that she couldn't drive or get out of bed. Now she receives a shot every three weeks—"basically," she explains, "to put me in medical menopause until we decide what happens."

Alice sees her recent experience of having a condition that gets progressively worse as similar to someone with multiple sclerosis (MS). She reflects:

I look at myself as a paraplegic and then I think about people with MS and I think, what's tougher? To go through a progression or have something drastic? I think [for] myself, I would rather have had the drastic . . . than the progressive [disability]. I can't imagine the pain of slowly going through it.

She feels that it is difficult for the able-bodied to understand how to help someone who is disabled. She recalls that when she started to go out for activities and wanted to take swimming lessons, she found the instructor, who was able-bodied, not helpful. She asks, "How can she know how my legs will be? How can you teach a paralyzed person to swim when you're not paralyzed?"

However, Alice is not very sympathetic with disabled people who get angry when someone asks them if they need help. "I think the person who is disabled shouldn't be so defensive," she says. "I've known a lot of people who were angry from the beginning, so they would be the type to yell if somebody asked if they needed help."

She went on to reflect that some people, like the actor Christopher Reeve, who is a quadriplegic from his riding accident about nine years ago, are focused on a cure. She says, "He keeps saying, 'I'm going to walk, I'm going to walk.' I think that's what gets him through the day. But you know what? If you keep waiting for that day, you're going to miss your life."

Alice adds, "But if that's what gets him through, then God bless him." She concludes, "The bottom line, Mary, is that it's very sad that it took a celebrity like Christopher Reeve to open everybody's eyes, to fight for more research on spinal cord injuries."

Alice thinks she has changed since becoming disabled. She says, "I was a nice person then, but I think I've improved! I wasn't a very bad person at all before my accident, but I think I'm twice as good now! I'm sensitive to other people's needs. And [I want] to help the next person, especially another woman who is paralyzed."

Alice was critical of the medical world's lack of specific knowledge about her condition and other disabilities. She says, "There are not enough doctors who have spinal cord knowledge. I'm not talking primary care; I'm talking urologists, neurologists, down to eye doctors. You take medication. It deteriorates your eyesight, ruins your teeth. They need to be taught or have access to knowledge about these things."

But even more than doctors' lack of training, she criticizes their failure to listen to their patients—a theme noted by Elaine and others I interviewed. She says:

Most of the people I know who are paralyzed are very in tune with their bodies. I am. I listen to my body all the time. And to these doctors, I would say, "I know my body better than you. Take my word for it. Use what I tell you." It's really hard to find a doctor who respects that.

In a rare moment of complaint, Alice says, "I think able-bodied people take minor things for granted. Ohhh . . . to be able to stand up and get a real hug. You know? I can't even imagine what that feels like anymore."

Alice, at thirty, has some goals she would like to reach in five years. She says, "By the time I'm thirty-five, I'd like [to have gone] back to school and I'd really like to have my own house—and a bunch of animals. Eventually, I'd like to have a career where I'm making a good salary so I'm comfortable. And I'd like to travel—I'd *love* to travel!"

At the end of the interview, Alice added one more goal: "You know, I've often thought I would love to write a book or have somebody write a book for me—about the trials and tribulations that I have been through." Perhaps this account will be the start of a longer story she will write herself as she continues to work out the challenges and celebrate the achievements of her new life.

2 The Way the World Sees Us

In her important study of hereditary deafness on Martha's Vineyard *Everyone Here Spoke Sign Language* (1985), Nora Ellen Groce points out that "the perception of a handicap and its associated physical and social limitations may be tempered by the community in which it is found."[1] In the Up-Island towns of the Vineyard, where hereditary deafness had existed for more than two hundred years and almost everyone knew sign language, she discovered that the residents, who remembered the community as it was, did not think of the deaf members as disabled. When she asked one woman about what she noticed as a child about those who were handicapped by deafness, the woman emphatically replied, "Oh those people weren't handicapped. They were just deaf."[2] Groce concludes in her study that a society can adjust to disabled individuals "rather than requiring them to do all the adjusting," since disability is "an arbitrary social category."[3] Her conclusion and its practical extension concur with the basis for disability legislation, which recognizes that the disabled have a right as citizens to full participation in society without discrimination.

Unfortunately, as Groce herself notes, the Martha's Vineyard perception of the disabled is rare, especially for a whole community. Usually society depends on validating its own perception of "normality" by contrasting it with those who are designated as "other" and then stigmatizing them.[4] The reaction to this stigma varied among the women I interviewed from confrontation to a temporary denial or "passing." A variation of these reactions is reflected in the American deaf community, which is divided into two groups. One rejects the notion that they are disabled. Rather, they claim, they are a separate culture with its own language. The second group defines its deafness as a disability and is more likely to assimilate into the able-bodied world.[5] The two hearing-impaired women I interviewed considered themselves bridges between deaf separatists and the able-bodied world. One of their narratives is included in this section.

The women I interviewed in this project experience different kinds of stereotyping and stigmatizing simply because they have a disability, which as Groce notes is a socially constructed category. The six stories in this section are representative of those cultural attitudes. Some women complained of being categorized as helpless or dependent, despite their achievements and status. Others spoke of feeling "invisible" or completely overlooked by their peers. Sometimes they experienced low expectations even from parents regarding education, employment, or finding a marriage partner. More consistently, they often experienced a "double consciousness"—living as part of the able-bodied world but knowing that they were perceived as belonging to an unfit world of disabled people. These women's disabilities began at different times in their life—at birth or infancy, progressively in young adulthood, or suddenly from a trauma in midlife.

The first two narratives, from Helen and Barbara, who were both born with their disabilities—spina bifida and orthopedic problems, respectively—tell of growing up and adapting to their impairments. Both received excellent educations and entered the professional world. Both also periodically discovered that their identity was defined and constructed by their disability. As Helen said, "You are put into this box." Barbara, a scientist, had to confront her mother's fear that she would not be employed or find a husband. In her professional life she felt more discrimination from gender than disability, but even so, when working with groups on issues of equity, she felt invisible and found her colleagues unaware of the needs of the disabled. Like Elaine and Virginia in part 1, these two women were drawn to work that would educate the able-bodied world. They became advocates for disability rights.

June, born with dwarfism, was fortunate to grow up with a family and a support group that protected her from feeling different. Employed in a civil rights office, she handles issues of equity in schools and also does advocacy work for the Little People of America. She thought about disability differently when she became the mother of her adopted son, who is also a dwarf. Since then she has experienced the shock of the world's stereotyping of him. Now, as a mother, she sees "two worlds colliding"—the able-bodied world her son must negotiate and the loving world she can provide.

Robin has experienced another version of living in two worlds. The gradual development of multiple sclerosis in her twenties has led her from occasionally walking with a cane to getting around exclusively in a wheelchair. Her professional life as a historian changed because of her altered physical condition. After taking time off from a successful academic career because of her health, she found it difficult to find a teaching position. She feels that she has faced more discrimination as a disabled person than as an African-American woman, and she sees the marginalization of the disabled as a civil rights issue. "Society is oblivious of our needs," she says, "[and it] needs to take the ADA [Americans with Disabilities Act] seriously."

Eleanor, born "profoundly deaf," has been part of both communities of hearing-impaired people. As a child she experienced a segregated education in a school for the deaf that insisted on "oralism"—teaching deaf children to speak—so they could assimilate, as much as possible, into the hearing world. At her Catholic women's college she discovered she could be part of the mainstream educational world and have friends who were not deaf. Finally, she went to Gallaudet College (not yet a university) and discovered "deaf culture" as she prepared for a teaching career. Eleanor is at home in both worlds and familiar with the prejudices of both groups. She is well positioned to understand the two deaf cultures as well as the double consciousness that many of the disabled experienced.

Finally, Carol has lived with a different kind of double consciousness. She has an invisible disability, the result of a car accident, which caused several debilitating conditions, including paralysis, muscle pain, migraines, and finally lupus. For several years, she tried to pass as able-bodied so she could continue working, but she lost several jobs because she couldn't keep up with the physical demands. After experiencing the medical world's demeaning dismissal of her illness as women's hysteria, she was eventually correctly diagnosed and found part-time work. However, her colleagues at work and even her friends often do not really believe she is disabled. They insist there couldn't be anything wrong with her because, as they say, "You look fantastic."

These women's stories often reflect the intersection of gender and disability discrimination, and they illustrate the difficult space disabled people inhabit between society's constructs of "normality" and "disability." The stories often express anger and defiance at this position. Like many other people with disabilities, they are not accepting their marginality. As Kenny Fries expressed it in his introduction to *Staring Back*, a collection of prose and poetry by disabled writers, "Throughout history, people with disabilities have been stared at. Now, writers with disabilities affirm our lives by putting the world on notice that we are staring back."[6] The stories of the women in this section also show how their defiance is often turned into energy for transformation and change.

HELEN

"You are put into this box."

elen was born in the 1960s with spina bifida. She uses crutches but gets around rapidly. She practiced law for almost ten years but is now pursuing another graduate degree in social policy so that she can focus on teaching and research on issues that relate to disability. Although privileged by class, ability, and achievement, Helen sometimes experiences the isolation and "otherness" that the disabled encounter. She uses the phrases "double consciousness" and "mixed identity" to describe her feeling of belonging to both the able-bodied world and the disabled world.

Helen came to my office at Emmanuel College for her interview. A vivacious young woman, she speaks rapidly, often breaking into infectious laughter. A year later I met her at a disability studies conference where we had lunch, and she brought me up-to-date on her graduate work and her involvement in the disability movement.

In our interview Helen described how spina bifida affected her from birth. At two days old, she had surgery to repair and cover with skin grafts the opening in her spinal cord. She explains that the nerve damage from the disease caused neurological and orthopedic problems for years, resulting in frequent operations.

She feels her family dealt with her disability very well, particularly her father, even though he was said to have fainted when they first told him of her condition. But she adds, "He was the sort of person who didn't expect everything to go his way in life." Her mother, who was high-strung, was more unnerved by things. Eventually, after her parents divorced, Helen went to live with her father when she was in fourth grade.

Her father was a very important figure in her life, she says. He was a successful businessman and an influential person in the small midwestern town where she grew up. She feels he indulged her, but at the same time he insisted that she be tough and try to do everything, even chores around the farm where they lived. She felt, in fact, that he brought her up as a son. Most important, he was always a booster to her ego and a fan of her achievements.

Looking back on her school days, Helen reveals a contradiction—a common theme in her story. On the one hand, she describes herself as a "strong-willed little girl" and "a very stubborn little girl" who "got used to a lot of attention" and perhaps "[had] too much of an ego." On the other hand, she describes a child who is not sure of herself and feels "different." She says, "I didn't fit in very well in a lot of ways and the disability didn't help." She adds, "I think people have low expectations for you as a little kid with a disability." She continues, "I hated it when people said stupid things to me. I seemed to understand that they were stupid, but yet I think I got accustomed to a very mixed identity."

Helen lived in a rural area, a town of less than a thousand people, a mostly working-class community. Her high school was consolidated with students from several small towns. She was an upper-middle-class child whose parents had high expectations for her, but she was not challenged academically and although she did well, she was bored "and probably didn't do as well as I could have."

"[The school] got a day off for deer season," she remembers. "Half the school would have been in the woods hunting, so there was no point [of having school]." Academic achievement was not cool, she says. "It was not cool to be a bright, competitive girl." She adds, "You know, being a smart girl can be difficult. It pissed the boys off. I thought I was being playfully competitive. I thought, you know, I was just joking but it pissed people off. But I also think I was proud of the fact that my SAT scores were good."

In addition to being an outsider as a competitive girl, Helen had to endure the stigma of wearing leg braces until she was fourteen, a particularly painful experience for a teenage girl. She hated braces then and still does, although she sometimes wears a brace on her right foot, but adds laughingly, "I've been stubbornly refusing to wear [a brace] on the left foot. I'm being stubborn. I realize that, but I don't care!"

Despite very little academic encouragement from her high school, Helen was one of the 10 percent in her class who went to college. She got into Harvard, though she actually preferred Oberlin's more relaxed atmosphere. However, her father, who had gone to Harvard, would not hear of it and said, "I won't pay for it." But it was her stepmother's words that convinced her: "If you don't go there, you'll always wonder what it would have been like."

Although Helen wonders if she might not have been better off at Oberlin, she acknowledges that at Harvard she was socialized to the intellectual and social life. She describes her first reactions to college:

"I had real competition. I was not accustomed to that, and I was really disoriented. These kids were much more sophisticated. I remember calling home in tears: 'Everyone here is so interesting and I'm so boring,'" she told her father. "'Tell me something about me that's not boring,'" she insisted. When her father reminded her that she went to Europe, she said, "Everyone here's been to Europe; they've lived in Europe. My roommate told me she studied at the Sorbonne and I didn't even know what it was."

Like many small-town students, she had to catch up. She found some friends freshman year who helped her regain confidence. She says, "One, in particular, a guy from New York, the smartest kid in the whole class, liked to debate with me. We got along." She remembers, "He was used to being smarter than everybody else, so the fact that he was smarter than me didn't bother him. We would have these debates about Kant and Kierkegaard, and if I didn't know who somebody was, he'd just tell me." She continues, "He'd say to me, 'Well I could tell *you* were very smart. You just weren't educated.'"

Helen, an English major, feels she didn't make as good use of her academic education as she could have, but as she says, "I was still learning how to have friends." In her sophomore year, she recalls, her roommates were a group of girls "who kind of took me under their wing a little." She had a couple of dates her freshman year but didn't really like either of them and wasn't that desperate to bother with them. She recalls, "I never thought I fit in with any group completely."

Her college years were interrupted by three more orthopedic operations. In one of her hospitalizations she developed a crush on her young resident surgeon, who knew his English poetry.

"He came by every day," she recalls, "and we talked about poetry and poets. And of course I developed this huge crush on him. He clearly liked me and kept coming to visit. On the last day, he came in and said [in Shakespearean pentameter], 'Shall I compare thee to a summer's day? / Thou art more lovely and more temperate [etc.].' And nurses were there and we clapped. So this gave me more confidence."

In fact, she recalls, it emboldened her to ask out a lawyer with whom she worked as an intern at a legal services office. He was twenty-eight; she was twenty-one. He was also disabled, with muscular dystrophy. Now, she concludes, "The relationship was not that good for me ultimately. When I look back on it, I think he was a very confused person."

Helen took the internship in the legal services office because she was thinking of becoming a lawyer so she could do advocacy work for people with disabilities. After graduation from college in 1984, she applied to law schools and was accepted at one in Chicago.

She had clearly made it into the mainstream in achievement despite her disability, but she remembers that "a sense of isolation still can persist." Law school was a real challenge intellectually. She says, "[It was] probably the first time I really had an academic curriculum that I found truly difficult. I mean really hard. College was hard, but it wasn't extraordinarily hard. I could always get by. Law school was the first time I really couldn't get by." But she did get by. Although in her first semester she did poorly, each following semester she did a little better. "I think it was the first time I really worked," she recalls.

After graduating from law school in 1987, she went home to study for the bar exams in two states and passed in one, then retook the other and passed that, too. While she was waiting to hear about results from the exams, she went for a few months to Guatemala where she became a teacher's aid in a school for the disabled. Her trip was suggested by a mentor in a disability law and health center where she had volunteered while in law school. She wanted to improve her Spanish but also, as part of her growing interest in public policy, she wished to learn about "how people with disabilities fare in another country."

Her father had become ill while she was at home studying for the bar exams, but he insisted she go. Tragically and unexpectedly, he died a day before she arrived back home. After staying at home to settle his affairs and recover a little from the shock, Helen took a job in legal services in Chicago, following her plan to do public service law. She stayed there two and a half years representing people on social security disability and Medicaid, among others. Following that she was employed at another social service agency for four years and then at a job in government, working on health insurance issues. Helen found that she was increasingly dissatisfied with the kind of routine tasks that her jobs required and that she was becoming more interested in research. She decided to leave the law field and start graduate work in a related field.

Helen admits she feels some ambivalence in her relationship with disabled people and the able-bodied. She has a foot in both worlds, she says. Sometimes she forgets about her disability, and sometimes her friends seem to forget it, too. But, she adds, one day when you feel comfortably part of the mainstream culture, you suddenly encounter an incident, maybe small and insignificant in itself, but symbolically enormous to you, which puts you right back into the world of the marginalized. She gives an example of such an incident that happened to her.

The incident occurred when she was working for a government agency and staying late one Friday night. She was talking to her boss and getting very positive feedback. He said that things were going very well, and she remembers that she was really pleased. A male boss was acknowledging that she, a woman lawyer, had done a good job. She felt that her professional life was thriving, and so was her self-esteem.

She left the office and got to an intersection, which at this point in the evening was not busy with traffic. Helen's account follows:

There were no cars, none, zero. I'm walking toward the intersection and this big, tall woman is walking toward me, and just as I was going to cross, she bounds toward me, and she looks at me and says, "Why don't we cross the street together?"

Well, I was just livid. I mean, it was all I could do not to really scream at her. I remember my first thought was, "Why don't I beat you within an inch of your life?" That was my thought, you know. I really felt this rage well up within me.

I said, "I don't really look like I need help crossing the street, do I?"

She had this real "Lady Bountiful" air, which was one of the other things that really got to me. Somehow, being asked if I needed help crossing the street just pushed my buttons. And also I think I had been feeling so good and so confident, and here's somebody treating me like I was so incompetent or helpless.

I think all these stereotypes just crash right down around you. I think that you're put into this box.

Helen continues: "As we had this conversation, she walked across the street with me and I said, 'I really did learn to cross the street, you know, when I was a little kid.' And she said, 'But that intersection is so busy.' And I replied, 'Well, it is not busy now, is it?' And I think she actually got it. I saw her from afar a little bit afterward, and she kind of looked at me and smiled and nodded and I kind of smiled and nodded back.

"But I felt like she wasn't really looking at me or looking at the situation. I can't imagine I looked like I was anxious because I was in such a good mood. And she wasn't really looking entirely at what was in front of her."

Helen's account of this incident, as minor as it was, sums up much of what she experiences in dealing with the world around her and its perception of her disability. In the account, first she relives the anger and incredulity and surprise: "I . . . felt this rage well up within me." Then she further explains her feeling: "You're put into this box." After her conversation with the woman as they crossed the street, she describes a moment of understanding between them as they smiled and nodded at one another. But then her account goes back to the incident again, and she sums up the whole relationship: "I felt like she wasn't really looking at *me*."

Helen lives and works in the mainstream of society, but periodically she experiences the shock of being stereotyped and classified as marginal. As a woman, she shares the aspirations of many other women who want both a traditional family life and a career, but she believes that these goals are more difficult for a disabled woman to achieve, particularly a woman who is a highly educated achiever. Her account is echoed in many other disabled women's stories.

BARBARA

"You need to know that I feel invisible in this room."

ike Helen, Barbara has had her disability from birth. She was born with clubfoot, contracted knees, and other orthopedic problems. We met at her home where we sat at the kitchen table to talk and tape the interview. A small-statured woman of sixty-six, she was open and welcoming in our interview. Not only did she vividly tell her story about being a disabled woman scientist and educator, but she enthusiastically provided helpful information relevant to my project and interests.

Barbara has recently decided to retire from her full-time position at a museum, but she is going to continue consulting on a part-time basis. She uses an electric scooter when she goes to work so that she won't have to walk long distances. A bad break in her leg some years ago was a turning point in her physical mobility. Her recovery was slow, and she was left with more limitations in walking.

She began by talking about her childhood.

The public stigma of disability was felt in her family, particularly by her mother, "a very private person," Barbara says, "who didn't want people looking at her child and saying 'Oh, what a pity.'" She realizes it was difficult for her mother "to have this child who was some kind of spectacle as far as she was concerned." Her mother insisted on covering Barbara's long leg braces with big stockings, which made them even more noticeable. Her father, however, never seemed to be bothered by her disability. She had many surgeries as a child, was in and out of hospitals, and was often immobilized by plaster casts up to her chest.

"I was pretty lonely," she says. She had no siblings, only cousins, and she says, "I was never permitted to play with any other children with disabilities." Furthermore, she didn't go to public school until fifth grade. Until then, she was home taught. A teacher came to the house twice a week for about two hours, and she says, "The rest of my education was up to me." Barbara thinks that her early education was actually a good thing because it enabled her to learn how to think independently. Her parents were always supportive of her education. Her father frequently brought her books from the library.

From home learning Barbara went into a fifth grade "handicapped class" and experienced the segregation and stereotyping of the disabled in educational institutions at that time before the changes brought about by the disability legislation of the 1970s and 1990s. These classes, she says, with all the grades in one room, were always in the basement and were always next door to the class for mentally disabled children. The children would be bused to one school and then, Barbara says, "You would go to the room where, of course, you played Parcheesi all day." She remembers several children in her class with cardiac problems and three boys with cerebral palsy, but, she says, "There was really nobody like me." Nor was anyone in a wheelchair because the building was not accessible.

High school was different. The disabled students were all bused to the newer school that had an elevator and they shared the same homeroom, but otherwise Barbara was mainstreamed with the rest of the students. At this point she was able to walk quite well, so she could handle the enormous flight of steps leading into the school. However, a friend of hers, a young woman who had polio as a child, had to arrive each morning an hour before classes began, just so she could slowly and painfully mount the steps. Although the high school curriculum was not exciting and catered to a population that was not interested in learning, Barbara discovered her love of science in a chemistry class, which determined her future major in college and her field in graduate school.

Although her mother assumed Barbara would go to college, she couldn't imagine what kind of career she could have. Barbara remembers her mother's contradictory attitude toward her daughter's future. She quotes her: "Well, of course you'll go to college. I wish that you could be a schoolteacher; that would be a good profession for you. But of course you can't because no one would hire you."

Barbara adds, "She never really accepted the fact that someone with a disability can be a highly competent human being. She bought into that stereotype." She concludes, "I think she felt I would not earn a living, and she felt I would surely never get married."

In fact, Barbara married twice—"the first time," she says, "I think to get out of my house at the age of eighteen. And then again, for keeps in Chicago, in 1960."

The University of Chicago was where Barbara chose to do her graduate work in biochemistry, but first she attended Brooklyn College as an undergraduate, which she describes as a wonderful experience. She recalls the college as "a hotbed of all kinds of left-wing carryings on" but more particularly for her, as an exciting intellectual experience in an atmosphere of complete acceptance. "College was really the beginning of my life," she says. She found people who shared her interests and liked to do the kinds of things she liked to do. And the classes were fascinating. She felt no marginalization either as a woman interested in science or as a disabled person. On one occasion when she had returned with crutches and a cast after some surgery, she climbed up on a laboratory bench so that she could set up a chemistry experiment. When the lab instructor found her up there, he casually asked her if she was sure she could manage the course and then readily accepted Barbara's answer that she would be just fine.

Barbara started her graduate work in Chicago by getting a master's degree in biochemistry. She had to work full-time as a lab technician to pay her tuition and commute to the job at the other end of the city, so she didn't spend much time at the university. She soon discovered, however, the sexist behavior of the male faculty. The head of the department seemed terrified at the thought of a female wanting to do science—almost half of the graduate students were women—but her master's adviser was, she says, "an out-and-out woman hater." Most of the other male professors, she says, "saved their support and fellowships and suggestions for graduate work for the men." She recalls that although she has experienced discrimination for both gender and disability, in her professional life as a biochemist, sexism was the most pronounced.

On the other hand, Barbara liked the European style of her department. She explains their attitude: "It was very laissez-faire. You want to come to class? Sure, come to class. You don't want to come? That's fine with us, too. You will have to pass your qualifying exams somehow, and if you think you can do it by not coming to class, we don't care."

After finishing her master's degree, she did find a male professor who was very supportive, so she continued on for her doctorate degree, which she finished in 1965 with the help of a National Institute of Health (NIH) fellowship and teaching assistantships.

At this point Barbara did not find her disability an issue. When she took a job as a lab technician after graduating from college in 1953, it was not even mentioned. She remembers, "Nobody said to me, 'Oh, are you sure you can do this?'" However, Barbara recalls that her close friend from high school, the woman who had polio and walked with crutches and braces, did have trouble finding a position teaching even though she had graduated Phi Beta Kappa and received a doctorate in mathematics. She continues, "I think it was [difficult] simply because she was that much more visibly disabled." Eventually, her friend did find a teaching position, and recently she coauthored a book on the disability movement. About her own condition, Barbara laughingly concludes, "I was just on this side of scaring-people-disabled."

After receiving her doctorate in 1965, Barbara and her husband, also a biochemist, found postdoctoral fellowships in a university in Boston, each in a different laboratory. She stayed for five years as a research associate working on her own independent research related to the mechanism of enzyme action. She had no experience with discrimination in her department, but the campus itself, which was built on a steep hill, was not disability friendly. When she tried to get a special permit to park close to her laboratory, the parking officer looked at her and said, "If you can't walk, you don't belong here." She recalls looking back at him and saying, "We'll see about that." Of course, her boss got her the permit and reprimanded the parking officer, but the incident illustrates the mind-set of the general population before disability legislation made such blatant discrimination illegal.

Barbara's next job was doing research in the laboratory of a major hospital that was conducting a funded project on the thyroid hormone. Her boss, a physician, didn't like women scientists and was very open about it. He said, for instance, that she couldn't get a raise because he would give it to her male colleague, who needed it to support his family.

She recalls, "The man was breathtakingly sexist. He was just unreal. I don't know what he thought about my disability. Probably plenty, but he didn't figure out how he could squeeze that in."

Despite the unpleasant atmosphere, Barbara stayed in the job for eight years while her two adopted children were small and until the federal grant ran out on the project during the Nixon administration. Soon after, events converged to make her reassess her career. Her mother, on one of her visits, had a heart attack. A widow then, she stayed on to be cared for by Barbara's family. Not long after, Barbara broke her leg in several places and was laid up for a long time. In fact, she sees this accident as a major factor in her declining mobility but also responsible for rethinking her career interests.

She had often gone to her children's elementary school to help with the science curriculum. After recovering from her accident, she became more involved in science education and was hired in a school as a "scientist in residence," which she loved. Working with the teacher as a team, they brought hands-on science to the children, where all the students got to do experiments illustrating the principles they were studying. Barbara realized how much she was interested in the educational process. She remembered her own childhood education in elementary school and how wrong and unnecessary it was. She determined to use her professional knowledge to improve science education.

Around 1978, Barbara had become involved in disability advocacy. She helped the American Association for the Advancement of Science (AAAS) lobby Joseph Califano Jr., the secretary of Health, Education, and Welfare, to issue regulations for section 504 of the Rehabilitation Act (providing civil rights for disabled people in programs funded by the federal government). She remembers when the AAAS itself showed a new consciousness of the needs of its members with disabilities. At a meeting of the organization in a hotel that Barbara attended, she saw, for the first time, other members who were disabled, some of them in wheelchairs. The organization had finally responded to the scientists who demanded accessibility.

Putting together her work in schools and her activism for people with disabilities brought Barbara to another phase in her interest in science education. She had volunteered in the science museum for several years and did an accessibility study on exhibits, suggesting ways to change them to make them better for people with disabilities. She approached the administration with a proposal to write a grant for funding such a project. She thinks the museum personnel, who were very conservative about change, didn't expect her to get the money. But after she got a grant from the National Science Foundation, the project was undertaken. In 1987 she was the outside contractor for the job of adapting and changing an exhibit, a diorama of New England habitats. The success of the project surprised everyone, even Barbara.

She explains: "As part of the agreement I wanted an evaluation to happen. And that happened. Before the changes were made, people just came in [the room] one end and out the other, looking at the dioramas out of the corner of their eye. In an evaluation, if you asked visitors to cite one example of an animal adaptation to its habitat, less than 20 percent responded with anything sensible."

Now, however, she continues, after the changes, mostly involving accommodations for visually impaired people—for instance, displaying stuffed animals that could be touched—100 percent of the people interviewed could name at least one animal adaptation and 80 percent could name two. "The difference was astounding!" she recalls. "I didn't expect to have that kind of a dramatic impact on the actual information people were getting out of the exhibit." She adds, "That's the story of what is called universal design in which you make common-sense adaptations and create something that is really inclusive and [it becomes] a much more interesting and educational space for everybody."

The director of exhibits was equally pleased and excited about the results. "Making an exhibit space more interesting," Barbara says, "and getting more people in there, and having them learn what you want them to learn means everything. At that point, [the director] really stopped and paid attention."

As a result, Barbara had a new career of planning and developing exhibits, which she continued until retirement in 1999. Now she is working at the museum on special projects, related to the dissemination of the principles of universal design as applied to museum exhibits.

Progress, Barbara agrees, in raising people's consciousness about disability issues has been slow. In 1993 she was asked to be on the committee of the National Science Foundation where, as a member, she saw the CEOSE's (Committee on Equal Opportunities in Science and Engineering) overall picture of how minorities and women were faring poorly on receiving promotions, fellowships, and financial aid. As for people with disabilities, "Nobody was even collecting data on their level of participation," she says. And as far as she can tell, this is still the case. Resources for people with disabilities were close to "absolute zero." She says, "I spent three years on that committee just trying to get on the radar screen of these people who were all supposed to be so aware of issues of equity." Finally at one meeting, she said, "You need to know that I feel invisible in this room. I and everything I represent and everything I care about in terms of equity." After confronting them, one member apologized for their unawareness and the committee vowed to do better.

Barbara continues to be an activist, fighting to include people with disabilities in the mainstream of society and to give them equal opportunities to live and work.

JUNE

"[I have seen] two worlds colliding."

June came to my college office for her interview with her adopted son, Michael, who was seven years old. He was a charming, curly-haired little boy, full of curiosity. She called him back into sight from time to time if he wandered off. But usually he played with his toys, talking to himself, lost in his own world. I gave him a coloring book and some lollipops, and he had his own supply of snacks. Like his mother, Michael was born with dwarfism. He looked like a child of about five, but he was still smaller than his mother whose stature—about four feet or so—would identify her as one of the "little people." Our interview focused on her life—growing up, going to college, and getting a job—but near the end of our talk when she mentioned a few of her experiences as a single mother of a dwarf child, I realized she had another story to tell. I kept in touch with her and, some time later, she sent me an essay she had written for a survey about parenting in the newsletter of the Little People of America (LPA). But I'll start with June's story before Michael came into her life.

June was born in 1960 in a little town in northern Maine. Her mother was a psychologist, and her father was a teacher and guidance counselor. She has one older brother. She says her parents did not know of her dwarfism until she was six weeks old, although today doctors are able to identify the condition much earlier. Now her parents see the delay as a plus, she says, because they had already bonded with her before they knew anything was "wrong." She says, "It took them a few years to totally come to terms with [her dwarfism], not blaming the world or God or anybody, but just being happy with the status quo." One of the reasons that her parents adapted so well to her condition was their involvement with the Little People of America, an organization that June praises for bringing together the needs of both the family and the children affected by dwarfism. They teach parents and family members that their children can live richly fulfilled lives. June explains how it helped her parents:

> Their idea before we got involved in LPA was [that] maybe I could work in the back room of a library somewhere and I'd live with my brother, who is a year and a half older. As soon as we got involved in LPA they realized that I could do almost anything. So that really helped.

June also credits her supportive upbringing to her parents being well informed. She says, "Once they knew there were options, which, you know, they hadn't really learned from the medical folks [in the early sixties], then their professional backgrounds ensured that I would be steered in the right direction."

June was mainstreamed throughout school and was able to participate in all kinds of activities, with minor modifications to accommodate her limited walking ability and other limitations due to her size. At that time, the schools did not make any provisions for disabled students, so her family arranged for such things as extra books at home (so she wouldn't have to carry them) and special arrangements with the buses. Since she lived in the same town all through school, everyone knew her and she felt accepted in the community. Perhaps, she recalls, there was some teasing and no one ever believed her age when she told them, but she feels that the combination of being mainstreamed and having the LPA as another supportive social community made her adolescence relatively easy.

When asked if all the members of the dwarf community acknowledged their condition as a disability, June says that many of them do not. However the LPA, which represents only 10 percent of the dwarf population, does acknowledge dwarfism as a disability. It takes this position because of the ADA's legislation, which now includes protection from discrimination for that group.

June chose a college in Boston that was close to the university her brother was attending. She helped to pay for it with grants. She says, "My parents joked that [I] chose it because it was halfway between Fenway Park and the Children's Hospital." She has stayed, she says, around the general neighborhood now for over twenty years. The campus was compact, which helped her walking problem, but she did have to think carefully about planning her schedule and what dormitory she could live in that would be convenient to her classes. She explains:

I chose a dorm that I remember measuring on a little map in the bulletin. I was trying to figure out which dorm was closest to the building for freshman classes. I remember being unpleasantly surprised that the dorm entrance was actually on the other side, so that meant it was like a third longer [walk to the classrooms].

She soon found, however, that she could increase her physical endurance. She says, "It's totally different from suburban life, where you just occasionally walk the long distances." Whereas before she got to college, she could walk only about three or four blocks without resting, she found, with more practice, that she had increased her mobility in the city. One Friday night she and her roommate walked all the way to her brother's college dorm and surprised him. He was amazed that his little sister had walked a mile! She notes that mobility for dwarfs is often limited because of spinal problems, particularly if they have trouble with their weight. Fortunately, she is slim, which, she says, gives her an advantage, though she can still develop back problems.

June planned to major in human services, but ended up in management because of the difficulty in finding an internship, which is a major part of the university's cooperative undergraduate program. During the sophomore year, students start an internship or "co-op" on or off campus that lasts for the full academic quarter. After being turned down for a number of co-ops, including one in the library, which she felt she could certainly have managed, she went back to classes and started again in the spring to look for one. This time she found a placement through a finance professor who was training stockbrokers and needed an office assistant. She says, "I stayed there for several academic quarters. And under the tutelage of these right-wing guys—these stock market guys—I changed my major to business or finally, to management." In the second half of her college experience, she had to catch up with all the business courses she needed, using her first two years of courses as electives. She adds, "I just thought for a while I wanted to do business, but it wasn't me."

Fortunately, within five weeks of graduation in 1984, she found a job at the Environmental Protection Agency (EPA) through a family she knew in LPA. After that she worked with a woman in an affirmative action compliance program and got involved as a counselor with the Equal Employment Opportunity Commission (EEOC). Finally, in her last job change, she applied for a job in the Office for Civil Rights in the U.S. Department of Education. She has stayed in that job doing technical consulting work for civil rights in schools and colleges. She hears complaints and analyzes the legal implications. Two-thirds of them, she says, are disability oriented, and many are elementary or secondary school special needs cases—questions of accessibility, for instance, or of denial of school activities, such as a field trip. She says, "There are parents and kids with physical disabilities who are still fighting."

I asked June if she informed potential employers of her disability before her interview. She says that her résumé would alert them because of her involvement with the LPA. She was very politically active in the organization as well as in other disability groups. "I was the New England director [of LPA] and then the chair of the national conference." She adds, "That was as valuable a work experience as the co-op job because I was negotiating with the hotel and different contractors [for services]." In fact, she considered the idea of taking a job at the Marriott hotel chain but decided against it because the company moves their employees around constantly. She decided to stay where she is and says, "Now I'm locked in the government."

June is satisfied with her work and receives good benefits, including health coverage. However, when I ask her if she has thought about future career changes, she says she would like to get back to Maine and maybe buy a house there. Her dream job, she says, would be either a consultant or the coordinator of the school compliance programs (section 504 of the Rehabilitation Act) in the Portland, Maine, school system.

One of the reasons June dreams of a house (she owns her condo in Boston) and job in Maine is her desire to provide Michael with a good life—and Maine represents that to her. She adopted Michael when she was thirty-seven and knew she wanted to adopt a dwarf child. He was profiled in an LPA newsletter as a five-year-old Latvian orphan, and she felt she could be comfortable with a school-age child. In her essay about being an adoptive parent, she notes that she has faced some of the same issues with Michael that she, as a disability advocate, had discussed with parents, educators, and the media.

She writes, "Over the years, I have often talked about the importance of making sure dwarf kids are treated according to age—not size—by family, school staff and peers. There are dwarf kids who sometimes learn to take advantage of the coddling and special treatment that is afforded them, and if babied, start acting younger, more like their size [than their age]."

June goes on to say that at times Michael has been in that situation where his maturity is more in relation to his size than his chronological age. She explains, "He started kindergarten three weeks after he arrived here. We live in an urban area with a high immigrant population, so his not speaking English was not unusual, [but because of] his tantrums and hyperactivity and being small and cute he was treated like a younger kid by his peers."

She explains that his maturing has been a slow process, which takes patience. She tries to balance challenging him to act at his age level with letting him act at his own comfort level. For instance, in his first year with her, she enrolled him in a preschool Sunday school class and a YMCA summer day camp even though he was six. She wanted him to have positive, enriching experiences and avoid some of the inevitable frustrations of school. Since then she has kept him in age-appropriate groups.

Michael did not really notice his "difference" for several years, she says, until he lost his front teeth and matured a little physically. Strangers often mistook him for a toddler, but he was not bothered because he didn't notice. June notes that he insisted that he was going to be as tall as her brother when he grew up, but she says, "I didn't worry or harp on [the subject] because he was comfortable around other dwarf children and adults. I just let it evolve." When he began to become aware of being seen as different by his schoolmates, she talked to him about his experiences. For instance, when he complained that the other children were not playing with him on the school playground, she pointed out to him that the others liked games and he preferred to just run around. Or when he was upset that other children stared at him and asked questions about his size and age, she helped him decide on a strategy where he would respond, "I'll tell you if you will give me a dollar." That seemed to him to be a good answer.

To help him feel at ease with his peers, June started to choose his clothes more selectively even before he noticed what other kids were wearing. She abandoned the T-shirts with Winnie-the-Pooh and the Velcro sneakers with cartoon figures, although she had to get slip-on sneakers because he still lacked the finger dexterity and patience to tie his shoes. He is in special education classes, though she doesn't feel he has a learning disability. As she says, "He just needs time to catch up." For her, it has been a "mind trip" to help him grow up. She says, "The advocate has become a parent."

June has experienced a double dose of stereotyping from the world's perception of her and her son as dwarfs. She recalls an incident in her twenties when she was walking back to her college campus. As a school bus passed her, some of the children called out, "Midget Mama." Although the "M" word is the most offensive, she found it amusing then to be identified as a "little mommy" rather than a girl or a woman. On the other hand, when she became a mother she felt differently about the way the world might perceive her child. As she says, she has seen "two worlds colliding"—the safe world she provides Michael and the world he must live in. She recalls once when she went to pick him up at school, Michael was in the middle of a circle of children, whirling around and clowning to amuse the onlookers. She snatched him away, horrified by the circus dwarf image that flashed across her mind. The children were not menacing and Michael was enjoying himself, but she felt a momentary fear for him and saw his disability as something she would have to negotiate with the world in a new way.

Male dwarfs, June says, often have more problems with social pressures because of the macho image of height. More female dwarfs marry into the mainstream population than their male counterparts, who, she says, are perhaps more vulnerable to issues of gender. When her roommate (who shares the apartment and is not a dwarf) paints her fingernails, Michael wants to paint his, too. June says, "I tell him, 'When you are sixteen.'" She adds, "At sixteen, he'll understand the consequences."

June is optimistic about Michael's future and his self-image. "Fortunately," she says, "Michael likes himself." He will be mainstreamed but will have the support of the LPA. He'll probably be slightly taller than she is, and he seems to be in good health. June would like to have adopted more children, but she had a recurrence of breast cancer recently—she had a lumpectomy in 1992—and it was scary to think of Michael losing another parent after having already lost two. Fortunately, it was not life threatening, but she doesn't think she would now qualify for another adoption. She is currently an "e-mentor" in the Orphan Foundation for a former foster care youth now in college, and she is very excited about this new role.

ROBIN

"I don't think any able-bodied person really understands what is involved in becoming disabled."

When I arrived at Robin's house, identified by a ramp out front which I gladly used, she greeted me with an air of excitement. She had received a phone call at 7:45 that morning from the head of the department at the university where she is teaching part-time. His message was that she could have a full-time position this coming year in her field of interest. It was wonderful to share the good news, especially because later I listened to her frustration and disappointment over the past year as she tried to find an academic teaching position. I followed her in her wheelchair to the kitchen, and we started the interview at a table shared by a friendly cat.

Robin, now fifty, describes the early symptoms of multiple sclerosis in her late twenties. She recalls the numbness and tingling in her arms, which she did not take very seriously. She was an undergraduate at Harvard, having taken ten years off between high school and college. She explains:

It was a political decision more than anything else. I graduated from high school in 1971, was fully involved in antiwar politics, and had enough of school by the time I got out. I spent those years mostly working in the music industry, which I got into through being hired by the *Real Paper* as a columnist in the 1970s.

The neurologist whom she consulted while in college did not tell her at first about his suspicion that she might have MS. However, when the symptoms returned and she was planning to go to England in her junior year on a grant, he provided her with the diagnosis and advised her not to go abroad or to go on to graduate school. She recalls, "I just decided I was going to ignore that advice and to the best of my ability, ignore the disease, which was relatively easy in the early years. My thought was that if I paid no lip service whatsoever to the disease, it would leave me alone. It seemed to work out OK for a while."

Robin continues, "Very gradually over time, I began to notice what are called 'MS episodes,' where you get worse all of a sudden. They began to be noticeable in that my gait would suddenly be very much affected." She began to use a cane more regularly, but in graduate school, which she started right after graduation with a B.A. in 1983 (she completed college in three years), and in her first teaching positions in the late 1980s, her disability was hardly noticed and was definitely not an issue in her hiring. She does recall an incident as an undergraduate when she entered a curriculum committee meeting using a cane and the well-known conservative professor said, "Do you really need that or are you intending to use it on someone?" His reference was not to her physical condition but rather to her political activism for undergraduates.

Robin's academic career blossomed. Although she didn't receive her Ph.D. until 1990, she was hired in 1988 by the Massachusetts Institute of Technology (MIT) as a lecturer in British studies and African-American studies before she finished her dissertation; the next year she was offered a chair in her special field of British imperial history at another college. After trying the new position for two years, she decided to return to the history department at MIT and stayed there as an assistant professor until 1995.

Except for recurring "MS episodes" and her use of a cane, Robin's disability was contained during those years. She notes that she felt discrimination as a woman and particularly in her department as an African-American woman interested in the position of black women in academia. In 1994 she organized a conference bringing two thousand black women to the campus. Although the administration appreciated her achievement, the history department thought it was "a great waste of time." She says, "They didn't see it as a scholarly exercise at all. And they made it very plain to me that they had considered that I had jeopardized any chance I would ever have at tenure."

After getting this message, Robin looked for another job and got several excellent offers. She says, "I figured there would be other universities that would appreciate someone like me. And sure enough, I wound up—much to my surprise, because I had not expected to like it—at the University of Texas at Austin." She continues, "I loved that job. The four years I spent there were tremendously rewarding. But it was also very bad for my health because Austin is a hot place. Heat is very bad for MS. I knew that going in, but I was feeling invulnerable, I guess, and I decided that [because] I had beat the disease all these years, it wouldn't catch up with me."

She found everyone there to be kind and helpful and the history department, which was large, very sympathetic to her interests. She explains, "A full third of the sixty-five [members of the department] were working on race and ethnicity in one way or another, which is my field of interest. So I always had people I could talk to about what I was interested in."

Not only were her professional expectations met, but Robin also found that students, colleagues, and graduate students looked out for her. She had used a walker for three years but then changed to a wheelchair, which took less energy to get around in. The campus, with forty-eight thousand students, was huge, so getting from one place to another was a challenge. But, she says, "My graduate students, for the most part, were pretty good about remembering that most of the places where one could get lunch were out of my range. So they would get lunch for me." They also met the challenge of difficult classrooms. She recalls:

I had a big 150-person lecture course on African-American history. And they put me in a classroom that had just been renovated—one of these tiered deals where the professor is in a well at the bottom. They had left spaces at the top for handicapped students, but [there was] no way for a handicapped professor to get into the room! So two male graduate students would cart me down this tiered thing in my wheelchair three times a week: up and down, up and down, up and down. Never dropped me once!

It took about three years for the climate and a vulnerability to allergens to hit Robin. She ended up in the hospital with a massive sinus infection from cedar pollen. She says, "[It] gave me a 104-degree fever, and I had to be scooped up off my floor by EMT guys and trotted off to the hospital. And nothing was ever really the same after that." It was with regret that she took a two-year leave of absence from her job and decided to go home to Boston. She took a position as a director of multicultural affairs in a prep school in New England, thinking that getting housing close to her employment and having access to a dining hall would be practical. Cooking had become difficult for her because her hands, particularly her right hand, were affected by the MS.

Robin's job at the prep school turned out to be a disappointment. She feels that the school did not take her job seriously. She explains, "They refused to institutionalize the position. I never got an office. I never got a telephone. I never got the kinds of things I needed from them just to do the job." She also felt patronized as an African-American. She remembers, "Whenever I ran into the headmaster's wife, she would tell me about some person of color whom she'd just discovered whom she thought was fabulous. Every single conversation would start this way."

But Robin maintains that the worst discrimination she has experienced has been as a disabled person. She says, "All my life I've been a black person, so I know what that kind of racial discrimination is. The discrimination that handicapped people face is worse." Her deteriorating physical condition has changed her attitude toward her body as well as her awareness of the world's perception of her. In the last year, she says, she has lost thirteen pounds—she is now at her weight at fifteen years old—and she is five foot nine. Now she is experiencing rapid transformations of her body. She can no longer walk nor write, so she uses her computer to receive and correct her students' papers. She explains that her mother, who comes to help her regularly, filled out the questionnaire I sent before our meeting. Her parents have been very generous in letting her have their house while they remain in their summer cottage.

Robin concedes that it took a long time to acknowledge the severity of her condition. She describes the turning point:

Like I said, I had this notion that if I gave lip service to the disease, if I acknowledged it at all, it would completely take me over, but I finally got to the point where I could not carry on with that and I would say that was probably when I went into the wheelchair full-time, which was three years ago now, four in September. I couldn't pretend that I could manage by myself any longer.

She continues by describing the particular frustration of a person who becomes disabled over a period of time:

I don't think any able-bodied person really understands what is involved in becoming disabled. I'm quite sure if I had been in some kind of catastrophic accident, where I had become a quadriplegic overnight, I would have had so much more help than I've had with this experience of gradual decline. Nobody offers to put you in a rehabilitation hospital so that you can get the knowledge that you need about how to cope.

She had her first positive rehab experience recently when she underwent surgery to implant a device that directly supplies a muscle relaxant to her spinal cord. She says, "I was [in the rehab center] for two weeks so that I could work with the rehab people. And they taught me things about getting around in a wheelchair that I had not known before."

An even more positive experience has been at an MS center where, for the first time, she has met a group of people with the same disability. She recalls, "I was in an infusion room full of people with MS. And that was a lot of fun. We were chattering away like magpies about our various experiences."

Robin's awareness of the world's attitude toward her physical impairments became clear to her in her recent job-hunting experience after leaving the prep school. She explains:

People look at you funny when you're in a wheelchair. I have a reasonably solid reputation in my field. I think I applied for six jobs in Boston this year, and I didn't get one single interview, which as far as I'm concerned is an enormous slap in the face.

Not even an interview. The only thing I could think of was that I had been really open and honest in my cover letters to these people about being in a wheelchair.

Society, she finds, is ill prepared to accommodate disabled people. She recalls that last summer when two of her former students visited and they all went to her favorite childhood ice cream shop, they found that the building was not accessible. "There are two steps to get into the place and the bathroom is on the second floor, which can only be reached by a stairway," she says. "I was horrified that they were doing business that way ten years after the ADA."

She has also been discouraged about accessible housing. She would like to move so her parents can come back to their house in the winter, but even a friend, who is a landlord, started talking about "grandfather clauses" that would exempt him from making renovations when she asked him about making an apartment accessible. In her attempt to get personal care help, she has experienced the familiar bind of needing financial help to hire attendants but making too much money to qualify for social security disability insurance. When she did contact an agency to hire someone, they sent her a different person every week, and one of the attendants stole money from her wallet. Daily she confronts barriers to mobility and transportation. She found that her town had failed to install adequate curb cuts for a wheelchair user. She describes her journey on her scooter each week to a therapist at a nearby hospital:

When the weather is good, I go up there by myself on my scooter, up Washington Street where there are very few curb cuts. So I have to go down the street to the first available driveway and then back up and down, and up and down. And that journey, from here to [the hospital], which would ordinarily be a ten-minute affair, has come to be emblematic for me of the whole disability thing. Our society is just not geared for people without legs. And that's the end of it. It's really the end of it. The able-bodied world would like to pretend that [the disabled] don't exist. Until such time as somebody begins to take the ADA seriously, and until such time as the "grandfather clause" is done away with,

I think life as a "gimp"—which is a word that I use—is going to continue to be rather more difficult than it needs to be.

Robin has experienced an awareness of the able-bodied world's obliviousness and ignorance of the disabled in her private life as well as in the public domain. She explains that when she finally admitted that she could not manage by herself any longer, she found that even people close to her could not acknowledge how much help she needs. Her parents, as she says, "still would prefer to think of me as being healthier than I am." And she finds that her increasing dependency is impacting her relationship with her male companion of fifteen years. She explains: "[He] won't even consider cohabitation in large part because he thinks, as I do, that part of the reason why we've managed to maintain this relationship so long is that we've never done that. We've always reserved space in the week for ourselves. We spend three or four days together and then have a little time off. It's always worked well." Some time ago, she says, they had made a decision, mostly political, not to marry.

Now, however, Robin's doctors tell her that to continue to live alone is dangerous. And even though her companion has been very sensitive to her predicament—"his nursing skills, since my surgery, have been extraordinarily improved," she says—it is a very different situation to be permanently dependent. She has thought about it a lot and says, "The fear of being stuck with an invalid. I can quite understand how that would be perturbing. I can't say, for sure, what I would do if the shoe were on the other foot. I'd like to think I know what I would do, but I don't know for sure."

Robin describes an incident that illustrates her predicament of living alone. Looking back, she finds it amusing, but it could have been otherwise if her companion had not been there:

"I went out one Sunday, about a month ago, to get the paper and wound up flat on my back at the end of the ramp. I don't quite know how that happened, but the wheelchair just flipped back, and there I was with my legs in the air." She laughs, "There were people who were jogging past me who seemed to think I was saying hello to them and kept going."

Fortunately, she had left the front door open, and when she started shouting, her friend heard her and was with her in seconds. She continues, "[The joggers] did turn around and come back when the image finally 'computed,' but by that time, he had already gotten to me."

Robin smoked as we talked, and as if by way of explanation, she commented that her mother loathes cigarette smoke, "but she has agreed to let me smoke in her house because she has finally figured out that I sort of need anything that gives me a little bit of relief." On a somewhat defiant note she continued:

I'm not overly concerned about lung cancer because I'm not crazy about the idea of spending another forty years in a wheelchair. So if lung cancer comes along, that's OK with me. I'm going to be fifty at the end of May. This disease [MS] won't kill me. It used to kill people, but it doesn't anymore. They've got ways to boost your immune system and deal with infection. So you don't die from MS anymore. But you can become completely incapacitated, absolutely. And the thought of that isn't thrilling to me either.

At present Robin is having chemotherapy with a drug that is supposed to slow down the process of the disease. It seems to be working, but it can be taken only for two or three years because of the side effects. "It's a time-buying device," she says, "in the hopes that in the next couple of years they will come up with something else that will work better."

Robin finished the interview on a note of determination. Despite increasingly difficult physical conditions and despite all that she learned about the way the world perceives her, she has no intention of giving up her career and her goals:

I spent too much of my blood, sweat, and tears to get that Ph.D. from that male-oriented institution to give up at this stage of the game! I'm just hitting my stride! I discovered this when I had a computer accident and lost fifteen years' worth of lectures. [Actually] they're not lost, they're just in storage. The question was: Could I do this [lecture] without my books and notes? And the answer turned out to be yes! I have reached the point where I know enough about what I'm talking about to just talk. Which was a great feeling! I'm not going to quit now!

When I thanked Robin for her time and spoke again of how glad I was to come the day she got the news of her appointment, she said, "It's very exciting. I called my mother immediately after he called me, and I woke her up. But she was happy to have me wake her up!"

ELEANOR

"I used to shut out hearing people and stay within deaf circles of friends, but I was wrong."

I met Eleanor through a mutual friend. We have become good friends since then, and I have had a chance to hear more about her remarkable life. Her life story spans an era of changing attitudes and opportunities for the hearing impaired—from her childhood when in a school for the deaf she was forced through "oralism" to imitate the hearing world, to her young adulthood when she discovered deaf culture and American Sign Language (ASL) at Gallaudet College and to the present when, as she says, "Deaf students are very fortunate to have access to learning with facilities provided." Born with profound deafness, Eleanor says she has turned down interviews in the past, but agreed to this one because of our mutual acquaintance.

Eleanor drove up from the South Shore, where at that time she lived in an apartment overlooking the sea, to meet me in my office at Emmanuel College. She is extremely proficient in reading lips and in communicating; I only occasionally had to write down something for her so that I could make sure I had understood a name or place. A trim-looking woman of sixty-six with very blue eyes and white hair, she punctuates her story with humor and expressive laughter.

In describing the origin of her disability, Eleanor recalls her mother saying that her deafness from birth in 1932 might have been caused by an injury from metal forceps, since there were red marks around her ears after the delivery. Eleanor describes her family's reaction as "shocked, heartbroken, helpless." She feels her parents didn't quite know what to do for her. She says, "I was a spoiled child. I had tantrums because I couldn't communicate, so they just gave me what I wanted." At the age of six, she was sent to the Boston School for the Deaf, where she boarded for eleven years, coming home for Thanksgiving, Christmas, and the summer. At that time, the Massachusetts State Department of Education required "pure oralism," a method in deaf education that mainly used lipreading and training in speech production instead of signing. This methodology had won out over sign language despite the opposition of many, including the National Association of the Deaf (NAD). Eleanor was taught to approximate speech, using her throat. She also learned to lip-read but, she says, for four years she didn't know what the words meant. Commenting on the forced oralism, she says, "Tragic! It is now a thing of the past."

Despite the rigid teaching, Eleanor remembers how the students improvised their own form of communication. She says, "The students at the school developed their own sign language and the older ones taught the younger ones in secret, behind the teacher's back. When they got caught signing, they were punished." Eleanor adds, "I was caught thousands—and more—times!" Later, when in college and doing an internship at the Boston School for the Deaf, she recalls showing students, after class, homemade sign language. "They loved it!" she says.

In parochial high school in Brockton, Eleanor was no longer with other deaf students and had to rely on the willingness of fellow students to take notes for her. Schools in the late forties and fifties had no accommodations for the hearing impaired. Trying to follow the classes by lipreading, Eleanor missed a great deal of what was being said, though the teachers thoughtfully asked everyone to speak slowly for her. She remembers those years as being very difficult because she was defined by her disability, not recognized for who she was.

One particular trauma stands out: being forced to take piano lessons and play in a recital. This was particularly hard for her, since many in her family—parents and relatives—were highly competent musicians. She says, "Imagine me, a pianist without hearing or understanding of music!" To this day, she remembers the event and the piece she had to play. It was called "Claudette." She says, "I was scared to death. I hated it and never played [the piano] again!"

Eleanor recalls that a nun, Sister Helen Marie, her eighth grade teacher from the Boston School for the Deaf, encouraged her to go on to higher education. Eleanor's goal was to be a fashion designer or to join the United States WACs (Women's Army Corps). With a partial scholarship and vocational aid from the state, she went to Regis College, which was an important turning point in her life. She majored in home economics, and although she was advised that she would not be able to get into the merchandise business or be accepted in the U.S. Army, one of the nuns, who had learned about Gallaudet College for the deaf (not yet a university), urged Eleanor to go there and prepare for a career in teaching.

Neither Eleanor nor her family had ever heard of Gallaudet. Founded in 1864, the college was "dedicated to the higher education of people who are deaf or hard of hearing."[7] In 1988, the students demanded that the president of the college be a deaf person. The success of the uprising resulted not only in the appointment of the first deaf president, I. King Jordan, but also in the recognition of the college's role in the disability movement and its place in "setting the stage for the 1990 Americans with Disabilities Act."[8]

Eleanor's family were overwhelmed when a representative from the college came to their house in 1957 and explained to them the concept of deaf education and American Sign Language. She says, "Mom, Dad, and my grandparents wished they had known about Gallaudet when I was at the Boston School for the Deaf and wished they had learned sign language so they could communicate with me in my early years and with my friends when they visited me at home." Eleanor recalls that she was often an interpreter for her deaf friends when her parents tried to talk to them. "I was a fairly good lip-reader," she says, "but my friends were not and needed to use sign language at all times."

Another important outcome of Eleanor's college experience, she explains, was her discovering friendships outside of her circle of deaf friends. Two close friends at college helped her to open up and accept the hearing world—"parents, cousins, friends." "It took me a long time," she says, "but they showed me the way." Now Eleanor moves comfortably between the two worlds and is often a bridge between the two cultures.

Eleanor spent a year at Gallaudet (1957–1958) after graduating from Regis. "It was very tough," she says. "I had to learn and use proper sign language [American Sign Language] and finger spelling." However, she also remembers that it was new and interesting, and she made several good friends with whom she has kept in touch. She traveled to Switzerland with one couple and their daughter, met their relatives, and hiked the Alps.

Her faculty adviser at Gallaudet encouraged her throughout the year and helped her find her first job teaching at Governor Baxter School for the Deaf on Mackworth Island in Falmouth, Maine. She taught fourth and fifth graders as well as typing to high school students for fourteen years. "[It was] my fondest and best time of working," she says, and recalls that the governor himself came to visit the school. She remembers him feeding corn to the many pheasants on the grounds and his enjoyment of his ninetieth birthday party that the schoolchildren gave him.

Eleanor says she has many good memories of her time at the school. "I participated in faculty shows—I was Mother Goose, and the students loved it. I coached the girls' basketball team. I feasted at the lobster bake on the beach of the island. I took the members of the graduating class on a field trip to Boston. I remember with other faculty members relaxing on a wintry Saturday in a tiny shack with a pot-bellied stove at the waterfront. Great memories," she recalls.

She found little mentoring during her graduate work at Boston University (1965–1966) where she earned a master's degree in special education and commuted from her job in Maine to take the classes. "There were no interpreters at that time," she says, and she again had to depend on willing note takers in her classes. "I missed many lectures and seminars," she recalls, "and had to read a lot."

Eleanor left her favorite job in Maine to take care of her ailing parents and then took a position, which she kept for seven years, at a school for the multi-impaired deaf and hard of hearing. This was followed by a job at a regular high school where she taught English, civics, and history to all of the deaf children. The students were with her in a "self-contained classroom" throughout their high school years, although they had interpreters for their other courses. She feels it was tough for the deaf children to have only one primary teacher for four years.

This appointment was followed by a job for four years as coordinator in a work-study program at the Boston School for the Deaf, placing and monitoring high school students. Finally, she spent eight years at the Horace Mann School for the Deaf in Allston, Massachusetts, teaching fifth grade math, high school history, and ASL to foreign deaf students, completing a career that required extraordinary flexibility, patience, and skill. Eleanor reflects that "thirty-eight years of teaching to the deaf has been a rewarding experience." She says, "It is a wonderful feeling to know that some students have been successful in their careers; they have become teachers, professors, professional artists, actors, and home builders. Foreign students developed self-esteem and some have entered the business world. Teaching instilled in me respect for all kinds of people and their diverse interests."

After retirement in 1996, Eleanor has pursued several kinds of work, requiring some different skills. She worked for a few months at Bell Atlantic and then took a job as a public service representative at Logan International Airport. She was working at Logan at the time of our interview. She explains:

I am back to work in a very different and more challenging environment that is not relevant to the deaf. My job is to help answer questions when departing and arriving customers approach and ask questions such as, "Where's US Airways?" or "Where's an ATM machine?" I wear a pin saying "Hard of Hearing"— actually I am not. I am profoundly deaf. Most customers notice and then talk slowly. That's fine!

She continues, "Sometimes impatient customers walk away in a huff. I don't despair at that. Anyway, I am having fun with coworkers. They have been wonderful!"

Sometime after our interview, I talked with Eleanor about her most recent change of employment. After leaving the job at Logan Airport, she took a course in basic computer skills and had an internship at the Environmental Protection Agency (EPA) for three weeks. She saw an ad in the paper for a part-time job, working from 1:00 to 6:00 P.M. for a group of public defenders in Boston. Deciding that this was the job she wanted, she immediately applied by fax without mentioning that she was hearing impaired. Several weeks later she got a call asking for her résumé. More time went by, and she discovered the law office, having noticed that her résumé listed her jobs of teaching deaf students, had contacted her computer program school and internship to ask if she was deaf.

In January she was given her first interview with an interpreter. She felt it had gone well, and she expressed her enthusiasm for working those hours. At the end of the conversation, the interviewer, with a solemn face, said, "We have just one rule that you should know about." Eleanor was startled and worried and wondered what it could be. The interviewer continued earnestly, "We do not allow anyone to come to work in a bathing suit." Finally she laughed, and Eleanor knew she had the job.

Eleanor says she enjoys the work—typing letters, faxing, copying, and doing other office work. Her fellow workers are easy to work with, and she feels welcomed by the whole community. She has been included in office parties and other events, such as a luncheon celebration for a promotion for one of the lawyers in her group.

Recently Eleanor and I drove down to the South Shore, and she showed me where she had moved into a subsidized high-rise apartment complex. It faces the highway on one side, but is landscaped and protected with a lovely park on the other side. She found that her apartment by the sea was too expensive and too far to commute to work. She says she is too busy to spend much time in her new home—"I am never there"—but it is convenient, and she can always drive to the shore when she needs to see the ocean.

We also went to see her old school, where she had boarded for eleven years. No longer a school for the deaf, it is now an institute for autism. Driving up the tree-lined driveway, I was surprised to find that the cluster of traditional red brick buildings did not seem austere or forbidding as so many of those institutions seem to be. She identified the different sections that once housed separate dorms for boys and girls, an auditorium, classroom areas (now mostly a parking lot), and playing fields.

In our visit, Eleanor confided that she had a special plan for her upcoming birthday: she was giving herself a special event. She was going to make her first sky dive and was, at that time, negotiating with a flying school that would take her on. I agreed that I thought this event would be an appropriate way to celebrate her seventieth birthday.

CAROL

"What do you mean there's something wrong with you?"

I met Carol in my office at Emmanuel College and, like the rest of the world, I would not have guessed that she had a disability. She is a slim, attractive, well-groomed woman who looks even younger than her forty-seven years. Carol is among many men and women who have an invisible disability. Since 1984 she has experienced a series of physical disabilities after a drunken driver broadsided the car in which she was a passenger. They include permanent muscle damage, joint disorders, cognitive problems of concentration and memory, and systemic lupus, which is possibly connected with the trauma of the accident. When we first met, Carol was struggling with anger and grief from the senseless and unexpected disasters that changed her life. When we met three years later, she was turning her anger into action and advocacy for the disabled and for disabled women in particular. I will tell her story as I first heard it, with a brief sequel at the end.

Born in 1952 in Keene, New Hampshire, Carol graduated from a public high school and began an ambitious life that included work, travel, and education. Studying at night, she received an A.A. degree and planned to continue studying for a B.A. She owned her own condo, had a savings account, and was happy in her sales and marketing job in a hotel. As she says, "Things couldn't be better." All this ended with the car accident. The immediate damage was a neck injury and paralysis in her hand and arm.

Although she was advised not to work and instead apply for disability benefits so she could take care of herself, she says, "I couldn't do that. My parents are low income. I had a mortgage that caused me a lot of stress and anxiety." She went back to work and attended a physical therapy program three nights a week.

She recalls, "It was really a complete life change for me." She was in a lot of pain and soon became aware of how oblivious people are to physical problems. Although she wore a neck collar and sling while riding on the subway, she found that no one offered to give her a seat.

She says, "That had such an impact on me. I remember hanging on to the railing in incredible pain. I'd feel like I was swinging on a pole like a monkey and [thinking], 'Can't these people see that I'm having trouble?'"

Eight months after she returned to her job, she was fired, which caught her completely by surprise:

The director of sales called me in one day and shut the door and said to me, "You know you don't fit the profile and the description of the type of person I want representing this hotel. I'm going to give you two weeks to look for another job and to leave."

I was in shock. I'd been there for two years. I said, "My performance reviews are excellent. What are you talking about?"

And he replied, "The way you walk down the hallway. You're really stiff. You're not really perky and energetic, and you don't fit the model of the sales rep that I want here."

I said, "Well, you know I was in a car accident. I'm doing what I can." And he answered, "I don't care what your personal problems are. I want you out of here."

Carol, however, found that she was a fighter and refused to leave. After contacting several people, including the organization Nine to Five, she was given the advice to write to the corporate office and argue that she had a temporary physical incapacity and that she loved her job and was good at it.

Her letter resulted in her reinstatement, and her director claimed she had misunderstood him. Later she heard that the corporation that owned the hotel was at that time facing a sex discrimination lawsuit brought against them by three women.

After a year, Carol realized she had won the battle but lost the war because she found that she was being overlooked for any promotions that came up. She left and took another job in marketing. In the interview, since she was no longer wearing a sling or neck brace, she did not mention her disability, although she was still experiencing weakness in her neck and arms.

Now came an even more difficult period in her life. Six months into the new job she asked to be excused from a special workday. Her boss had told the staff to come to the office the next day in work clothes so that they could help move heavy boxes from the basement. Carol explained that she was still unable to do physical labor because of her neck injury and she was excused. However, after that, she says, her boss's attitude toward her completely changed. She says, "It started a wave of harassment that I just could not believe." And it culminated in a humiliating experience when her boss sent her out for morning coffee and doughnuts (an errand usually done by an intern) and said to her in front of everyone, "Do you think you are physically able to carry the box back yourself?"

When Carol confronted him later with making her look like a fool in front of the other employees, he said, "You can only make yourself look like a fool if you are a fool." Three weeks later she was fired.

Carol recalls it was in June and one of the worse weeks of her life. Medical tests had just shown that she had severe nerve damage in her neck. Then her boyfriend of eight years left her. He said, "I've had it up to here with you and your physical problems," and he told her he was going out with another woman "who doesn't have the pain issue and is bubbly and healthy and can do everything."

Carol concludes, "[In one week] I lost my health, my boyfriend, and my job." She went into a severe depression. She says, "I spent the summer—June, July and August—totally isolated in my room, just going out three times a week for physical therapy. I would basically stay in my pajamas all day." She began to lose her friends, who would tell her to snap out of it and insist, "What do you mean there's something wrong with you? You look fantastic."

"My friends were angry with me," she says "because I could no longer be the person that I used to be." She continues, "That is the first time that I started realizing how judgmental people are."

Carol realizes now that she also was in denial about her disability. She refused to think of herself as having a permanent physical problem. She told herself that she would eventually get better and get a full-time job, so she wouldn't consider applying for disability insurance. Meanwhile, when her unemployment ran out, she lived on her savings for a while and then rented out her condo and moved into the attic room of a friend, putting her belongings in storage.

Carol's doctor told her she would probably not be able to work full-time again and urged her to get a part-time job. Despite fears of being fired if employers found out she was disabled, she started applying for jobs and looked especially for employment with health care coverage, which she had been without for a year. She found a twenty-hour-a-week job with health benefits at a state agency and finally, in her interview, she identified herself as having physical problems. "I changed on that," she says. But she was still shocked when her employers informed her that she was officially disabled according to the definition of disability in the state of Massachusetts.

Carol recalls, "That was really hard for me." She had to accept that classification, although she confesses, "I always thought I was just going to get better, better, better."

Unfortunately, her health got worse. She started having severe migraine headaches, and when she went to a medical center, she experienced the kind of dismissal that is often given to women: "Here's the situation," the doctor said. "You're single, you're not married, you're getting to middle age. You're bringing these headaches on yourself. This is all self-induced. I've seen this a hundred times before. You need to go into therapy."

Although Carol insisted, "If [marriage] was important to me I would have been married at twenty-two," the doctor prevailed, and she spent a year in therapy while the migraines continued. She was rescued by her physical therapist, who, after witnessing one of her migraines when she lay in a corner in a fetal position, insisted upon further examination. He discovered a dislocated jaw (brought on by the car accident) and explained that every time she opened her mouth, her jaw popped open. He told her to see her dentist, whose diagnosis was that she had TMJ (temporomandibular joint—a jaw joint disorder).

After the dentist tried to correct her condition with a bite plate, without success, Carol started a controversial treatment with a specialist. It is a nonsurgical procedure that gradually changes the bite by filing down the teeth until the jaw drops into its proper place. After the treatment Carol experienced an 80 percent improvement, but she had another battle to get insurance coverage, finally succeeding on appeal.

Listening to Carol's story makes you feel that her misfortunes just cannot go on, but she was still to confront another disaster.

As her treatment with the dentist neared its end, she began to experience unusual fatigue, but the dentist insisted it had nothing to do with the procedure and urged her to see her doctor. She put off going to the doctor, hoping her condition would clear up. But one day while shopping at a mall, she felt that she was going to faint. Leaving the checkout line and her full shopping cart, she went to her car, where she passed out. Two hours later, she woke up shaking and drove home at five miles an hour. She managed to get in the house, only to pass out again in the foyer, where she was found by a friend.

Blood tests revealed that she had lupus, which, her doctor explained, was a chronic condition, an autoimmune disease that as yet has no cure. Its progress could be slow or at times fast if it affected vital parts of the body.

Carol was devastated. She says, "That was another shock. Just when I thought I was going to get a good job and start making some money again and move back into my condo." She has found some support in a women's group in the Lupus Foundation of America, but the physical consequences of the disease have been severe. She explains:

When I was first sick, I could only be out of bed for about four hours a day, and then I would feel I'd been up for two days. My doctor explains it is like having an hourglass with sand in it. Everybody else's hourglass is five times bigger than mine. When the sand goes through, that's my energy. When the last grain of sand goes, my body shuts down.

Perhaps one of the most difficult aspects of Carol's experience with lupus is that it is another disability that is not visible. Despite her lack of strength and recent proneness to asthma and pulmonary problems, she still looks healthy and often encounters people's disbelief in her condition. She explains that this is a common complaint among the women in her support group. She says, "Everybody says the same thing. That people judge them and accuse them of trying to get favors or attention."

She continues, "We've had discussions and one person suggested that if you don't feel well a certain day, don't do your hair and try not to look good! But I said, 'Why should I try to look awful? What does a disabled person look like? Can you tell me? What do you want me to look like?'"

She adds, "Lupus is considered a woman's disease. [The Lupus Foundation] put out a pamphlet with a picture of a women in her mid-twenties. Very pretty. And it says in big, bold letters 'I may look healthy, but I am not. I have lupus.'"

Carol angrily described an incident that illustrates some people's attitudes toward invisible disabilities. She has a cot next to her desk at work so she can lie down if necessary. One day when she was talking to a temp who had been hired to answer phone calls, the young woman looked at the cot and said, "What is that with the bed?" When Carol explained she had a disability and fatigue from lupus, the temp said apologetically, "Nobody told me that. I know what lupus is [her aunt had the disease]. When I asked about the bed they told me you were spoiled."

Carol concludes, "I've had some really bad experiences. It really leaves its scars. I know I don't look disabled, but I have days when I can't get out of bed."

When I reconnected with Carol three years after our interview, she provided me with comments to some questions I posed and sent me two essays she had written, including one about her own experience with disability.

Carol writes, "I was tremendously angry for a number of years. I was not able to do many things that I could do in the past and I was in constant pain. I became depressed when I realized my condition was not going to improve and I would no longer be able to compete with my contemporaries. I gave up living. You reach rock bottom. I have been there, done that. It would have been easy to die. But some long-hidden desire to live surfaced within me. I convinced myself I was worthy of life. When I made that decision, I blossomed!"

She acknowledges that meeting a group of women who were disabled inspired her because they "did not allow disability to terminate their dreams and goals." They were role models that made her reevaluate her life. She made a decision to return to school.

Returning to school as a middle-aged disabled person was not easy, but Carol says, "The academic world saved my life. [The professors] bolstered my self-esteem and self-confidence. I was a wonderful student. I produced superior work."

At the age of fifty, Carol graduated from college with presidential honors, earning an award for academic excellence and becoming a member of Psi Chi, the national honor society for the study of psychology.

In another essay, she writes about her views on the need for the disability community to unite: "Lacking a strong unified voice, the disabled are not being included in diversity accommodations and are being left behind." She argues that disabled women, in particular, need to fight together for better recognition and accommodation: "Disabled women need to become empowered and not be reticent when it comes to standing up for their rights."

Carol and I had a reunion and met at Brandeis where I am presently a resident scholar in the Women's Studies Research Center. She still looks young and still doesn't look as if she has a disability. But she has actually had more health troubles. After a severe illness, she discovered that she had suffered a series of minor strokes and had CNS (central nervous system) lupus. It has resulted in some problems in short-term memory and in difficulty reading and processing words. Despite these physical drawbacks, she has become active in disability rights.

I asked Carol what she felt were the most important issues to address for disabled women. She says, "I believe respect and validation are important issues." She adds, "It is important for everyone to learn about disabled women in the workforce. We have our own unique needs and challenges that are being overlooked."

To work for these goals Carol joined the Diversity Committee at her agency. She says, "When I attended a meeting I was surprised to see that there were representatives from the black, Hispanic, gay, and lesbian groups, but no representative for the disabled. I mentioned this and was asked if I would like to organize a standing committee for disabled women." Carol organized the committee, and recently she planned and produced a very successful program for Women's History Month that spotlighted disabled women and won her a state employees award for "outstanding performance." She feels that perhaps her experiences as a disabled person have occurred for a reason and continues to seek to create a voice for all disabled women.

For her own empowerment, Carol has started a graduate program and hopes to get a degree in counseling. As for her personal life, she says, "It is my wish to someday live in an environment where I have some control—[a place] to decorate and to have my personal things around me. I would like to have a home of my own."

3 | The Way We Work

Unlike other minorities' civil rights bills, the Americans with Disabilities Act was not followed up by the implementation of affirmative action.[1] Or as one of the women in part 3 says, "There is no enforcement of the ADA. It is just a piece of paper." The high expectations that the disability community had after the bill's passage in 1990 have given way to disillusionment, as the decisions made by the U.S. Supreme Court regarding disability lawsuits increasingly favor employers. The Court has focused on the definition of disability—excluding more and more people—instead of focusing on the issue of discriminatory practices by employers. As Mary Johnson writes in an article in *The Nation*, "If disability discrimination is ever to be understood for what it is, the nation is going to have to begin to focus on the discrimination and stop obsessing about whether people are 'disabled enough' to 'deserve' protection from that discrimination."[2] She notes, "A decade after passage [of the ADA], disabled people remain as unemployed as they were, with 70 percent of all severely disabled people out of work."[3]

In *Beyond Ramps*, Marta Russell examines the reality of unemployment for disabled people. Writing about our society's work culture, which grants social status based on work, she warns against overstating the possibility of achieving full employment for disabled people under the current ADA legislation. She argues, "In reality there are disabled people who do work, there are disabled people who can work but who are prevented from doing so for various reasons, and there are those who cannot work."[4]

In part 3 I have selected the stories of six women that illustrate different work situations and the various challenges these women have confronted. Several of the women I interviewed were directly affected by the failure of the disability legislation, but that is not the only discrimination these women have faced. From poor counseling and inadequate educational opportunities to outright discrimination in hiring and physical and psychological barriers at work, their stories illustrate many difficulties. Nevertheless, these women are working or have worked—sometimes part-time and not always consistently—and they have achieved some measure of independence. Depending on what time in their life they experienced discrimination and how they perceived their disability, they have chosen to fight the discrimination, to adapt to conditions, to create alternate work situations, or to not work. Some are in wheelchairs while some are more mobile. They have had to find ways of coping with life activities as well as work.

Adrienne and Sally have both had professional careers and confronted discrimination, but at different times in their lives. Sally, who had polio at fifteen, virtually "passed" as able-bodied in the workplace for years and was not aware of discrimination until after she started using a wheelchair. In contrast, Adrienne, blind from birth, was "personally radicalized" by the discrimination she experienced when she applied for jobs in her early twenties after graduating from college. Brought up in a supportive family, she went to New York in the sixties expecting to find an exciting entry-level job. Her reaction to her rebuff then, as well as afterward when educational institutions rejected her, was to fight in every possible way, including litigation. Already an activist, she turned to disability civil rights and worked on disability rights legislation. With two graduate degrees, she at fifty-five now has a successful academic career and is a well-known bioethicist. Her work has been influenced by her political activism and her intellectual concern for social and ethical issues, which in turn have been shaped by her own experience with disability.

Sally experienced an almost complete recovery after her initial paralysis. She was able to complete her education and pursue college and graduate degrees in her field of food research. Her career was relatively unhindered by her disability until she had an elective operation for a curvature of the spine. The operation was mishandled and left her mobility impaired. She found walking with crutches difficult and ultimately used a wheelchair. Although her work continued uninterrupted, she recalls that attitudes changed toward her professionally and even her own self-image was affected. She realized for the first time that she was, in fact, disabled. She also became aware of the patriarchal discriminatory culture in her workplace for women in general. As her mobility decreased, she found it more difficult to maintain her own extremely demanding work ethic, so she retired at the age of fifty-five. Since then she has used her skills as an active advocate for people with disabilities.

Kristen, who had polio at age one, was more severely disabled than Sally and has used a wheelchair most of her life. Her story illustrates the difficulties of that position. Although she grew up with a strong self-identity and has a master's degree in rehabilitation counseling, she could not find adequate transportation to get her to a stable and satisfying job. She lives on supplemental security income (SSI) and speaks for many disabled women and men when she says, "If you have a visible disability, you're not going to get a job." Now, at fifty-one, she and her husband, who is also disabled, have finally financed a van that he can drive and that accommodates her wheelchair. Until recently they both were research assistants for an academic study on disability, but the project ended. Her story is a familiar one to many women: the challenge of combining home life, husband, and child with meaningful work. She chose to curtail her career and stay out of the job market partly because of increasing physical problems but also so that she could continue to raise her daughter. She knows that she would have more options to choose from if she had the support she needed.

Both Judith and Alicia have chosen not to fit into the traditional world of work. Judith, now fifty-eight, has created her own business, while Alicia, in her thirties, is studying art and lives on SSI. As a young adult, Judith developed multiple chemical sensitivities and Crohn's disease. She is unable to work full-time but has developed her own healing and fitness business. She has done a lot of thinking about the definitions of work and disability. Her experience of being unable to fit into the usual workplace convinces her that we need to expand our definition of work. Disabled people are kept from productive contributions to society, she says, partly because of the definition of disability in the social security system, which ties benefits to the amount of work a person cannot do. She feels she has found her own way and is interested in helping others become productive in the world.

Alicia has also redefined work to fit her needs. At thirty-eight, she believes in challenging and changing yourself and the world if it cannot adapt to you, particularly if you try to meet it halfway. She changed her old-world Portuguese parents' views of what a daughter can do and has found her vocation as an artist. Born with cerebral palsy, she attended a special school for the handicapped and found it constructive in handling her disability but weak in preparing her academically. She was typically guided into human services in college because of her gender, and she was counseled with little reference to her interests or potential. For four years she worked in community organizations with special needs children, but found she was not taken seriously as an adult. In art school she has found her direction, and she enjoys a community that doesn't treat her as someone to pity but rather as another creative human being. "We all have disabilities," she says, adding, "You need to believe in yourself and find your own life work."

Lauren, who describes herself as a workaholic, had to restart a successful small business career after an accident at age thirty left her with a spinal cord injury. She uses a wheelchair. Although she had to give up the flower shop she and her husband owned, she now works out of her home, producing dried and custom silk flowers for interior decorators and doing occasional freelance work in flower shops. Her fourteen-month-old daughter was born five years after her accident. Her attitude toward her disability was formed the moment she realized she had been severely injured from a thirteen-foot fall from a sea wall in Maine. She remembers thinking, "I understood what had happened to me, but I also knew that my life wasn't destroyed but that it had just been changed—dramatically."

These women have had to make hard decisions about their life and work. Some have had to give up hopes for "successful" or lucrative careers and accept dependence on meager government subsidies. Kristen chose to stay home and raise her child after finding the job market impossible. Judith, realizing she could not fit into a traditional work situation, created her own business, and Alicia took a chance on following her dream of becoming an artist. Others have had to restructure their life plans in different ways. Lauren had to give up her ambition of owning her own business and at least for now works part-time at home. Sally had to change her life as her physical condition deteriorated and she confronted a less supportive work environment. Finally, she had to make the decision to take early retirement. Adrienne decided when first confronted with discrimination as a college graduate that she had to oppose it, and that decision helped to shape her career and its development.

The stories of these women illustrate their determination to get on with their lives and show how much social and physical barriers and attitudes have affected their lives. Their strategies and creativity are typical of all the women interviewed.

ADRIENNE

"I love going to work."

I spoke with Adrienne on the phone and also in person, at the Wellesley College Center for Research on Women where I began my project. She is blind, a professor at Wellesley College, a well-respected bioethicist, and an expert on disability issues, including those of women with disabilities. A person who does not mince words, she gave me many helpful references and a number of caveats about the subject of my project. Later, we had a formal interview at my house after I picked her up at her office and we shared dinner together in my kitchen. Adrienne, who uses a cane, is an impressive figure—stately and self-assured. She was emphatic, clear, and eloquent in her narrative, as she is in her public presentations.

Born a premature infant, in 1946 in New York City, Adrienne says her parents "were glad I was alive. It took them some months to be sure that I was blind." Describing their attitude, she continues, "My mother says that she was very anxious at first. And my father, who in general is a very un-anxious person, just viewed it as something that had to be thought about." She explains their attitude further: "I don't think it [her disability] was an enormously loaded category called Blindness. It was like my sister was shy, and I was blind, and my brother was rebellious." She qualifies her characterization a little: "I do want to say that they made certain decisions based on the fact that I was blind that I think were actually very important and in general, very good decisions. So it affected certain things about my life and their life."

One of her parents' decisions was to move to New Jersey, one of the few states in the country that would permit blind children to go to neighborhood public schools and would provide books in Braille. In grades one through three, Adrienne had special classes in reading and writing Braille and doing arithmetic. She attended classes with the rest of the children in her grades for social studies, language arts, and the like. From fourth grade on, she was in the ordinary classes for the entire day and typed her homework assignments and her tests. After high school, which was largely college preparatory, she applied to three colleges and got into two, refusing the state college because she found the admissions interview "demeaning and insulting and infuriating." She recalls, "They were convinced I was going to get killed when I crossed Jackson Street [at the college]." Graduating from high school in 1964, she chose to go to Swarthmore College. Her blindness was not discussed at her interview.

I asked Adrienne if she had experienced much discrimination in her school and college years. She says, "Well, I had some discrimination in high school and some at Swarthmore, but usually I was able to battle it out and get my way. For example, in high school I had a couple of teachers who didn't want me in the class, but they didn't have any choice. They would say, 'I don't really think you're going to be able to do this work.' And I would say, 'Well, I'll do it and I'll find out. And if I can't do it, then I won't do it.' And I could do it. So that was that."

In college she also had a couple of professors who refused to let her take their courses. She would have fought them, she says, but felt she was not doing her best work and reasoned she did not have the leverage to fight. She explains, "When people were being discriminatory, I knew they were being discriminatory, but I also knew I didn't have the weapons with which to fight in my own heart."

Adrienne did feel good, however, about her other activities in college. She was a radical political activist, and she was involved in many musical groups. During the summers with high school friends in her hometown, she managed the groups, including the business arrangements, hiring the conductor, recruiting the singers and instrumentalists, doing the publicity, and getting the grants. So in 1969 when she and a friend took an apartment in New York City, she had high expectations that she would find an entry-level job in a nonprofit organization for the arts or for political/social services. Her experience in job interviewing was disastrous, however. She says, "It was beyond description. I [was] livid, heartbroken, betrayed."

Adrienne went on one hundred interviews in one month—all in organizations that she had respected, such as the American Civil Liberties Union (ACLU) and other foundations and nonprofit art groups. She was told various things. One was, "I'm sure you can do this, but I'm too nervous. I don't want to hire you." Or, "Even if you can do it, I don't want you here." Adrienne comments, "They were completely blatant about it. It was unbelievable." She describes one interview, in particular, at the Education Division at New York's Lincoln Center for the Performing Arts, which was for setting up concerts in public schools. She had a recommendation from a conductor with whom her music group had performed at the Lincoln Center, and as she says, "I had more qualifications than probably almost every other twenty-three-year-old they were going to get because I had been setting up concerts for ten years. She describes her interview:

> I went and had a meeting with the personnel director, and he said, "Well, you didn't tell me on your résumé that you were blind."
> I replied, "No."
> And he said, "I guess if you had I never would have let you come here."
> I answered, "Well, why do you think I didn't?"
> And he continued, "Well, you've convinced me, but now you have to convince the one you would work for and I'll see if she'll interview you."

"She wouldn't interview me," Adrienne says, "so I insisted, 'I'm not leaving this building until she interviews me.'"

"Well, [the building] closed and I left and came back the next day with a letter to the vice president that read, 'You don't have to give me this job, but you do have to give me an interview. I really have good qualifications. This is totally unfair. You have to at least give me a chance.' But they wouldn't [give me an interview]."

Adrienne found that there was no federal or state civil rights law at that time that protected people with disabilities from job discrimination. But when she called the New York City commissioner on human rights, she found that there was a city law, and so she filed a complaint. As a result, the Lincoln Center changed the job description, and after the commission did a totally inadequate investigation, it ruled against her.

Adrienne credits this set of events for convincing her that she would need to become involved in fighting for the rights of people with disabilities. She says, "I [was] so furious that I decided I was going to have to work to get a civil rights law [passed]. I realized that if I didn't do some kind of civil rights work for people with disabilities, I was never going to get a job." She became politically active and sought out other blind and disabled people, making new friends who were also fighting for their rights. This was, of course, before the major congressional disability legislation of 1973 and 1990. However, in 1974 Adrienne had the satisfaction of seeing the New York State human rights law amended to include people with disabilities, a campaign in which she had been a major spokesperson and organizer.

Meanwhile, out of her one hundred interviews for jobs, she took the first one she could get: typing at the Anti-Defamation League for B'nai Brith, a Jewish nonprofit organization. She also applied to the Columbia School of Social Work and three similar graduate programs and again experienced "an enormous amount of discrimination." The interviews, she says, were "nasty, paternalistic, and insulting."

When I asked Adrienne to further characterize her interviews, she explains that all they wanted to talk about was her blindness, how she was going to do things, and whether her blindness would bother clients. In short, she says, "It was all 'why did I have the right to be there?'" She got into three of the graduate schools to which she had applied, choosing Columbia and a program in community organization. She describes many other frustrating experiences in her graduate program. She had to find her own field placement because none of the field advisers were willing to work with her. When she did talk with one, the adviser asked her silly questions such as, "How do you manage stairs?" and insisted, when she did find her own placement, that she tell the organization that she was blind. Adrienne refused to do this and got the placement anyway. She concludes that no matter how angry and hurt she was for being so dismissed, she never doubted that she was qualified for what she was trying to do. Her anger galvanized her to continue to fight for her rights.

When Adrienne finished her degree in social work in 1973, she got six job offers, which, she says, surprised her because she continued to be confrontative and to demand that she not be evaluated or recommended with reference to her blindness. "Either I'm good at what I do or I'm not good at what I do," she explains.

I asked Adrienne if she had hoped to raise the consciousness of the people who interviewed or taught her. At first, she was adamant that she had not. "I wasn't attempting to raise anybody's consciousness," she says. "That wasn't my mission. I was attempting to get a job." She did finally concede that she might have made people think about disability differently.

Adrienne's interviews for jobs followed the same familiar patterns. She recalled that one woman, with whom she had good rapport, asked her if she managed her own household. Adrienne commented, "I felt as though I was watching the wheels turn. It was like, 'No, no, I can't ask who she lives with, that is an inappropriate question.' But what she wanted to know was whether I had a chaperone to pick out my clothes for me." She sums up the demeaning attitude toward her that she felt at the time: "I was twenty-six and [realized] that you could be a cute little child if you had a disability, but you couldn't be a full-grown adult." This was an attitude that many of the women in this project have encountered.

In September of 1974 Adrienne started working for the New York State Division of Human Rights as a policy analyst. As a volunteer activist she had lobbied state senators and had demonstrated at the state commission to support a bill, which she had helped to draft and which got passed. Now she was asked to help implement the law. She stayed for three years, reviewing case investigations and doing a lot of public speaking and many other things. She says, "It was sort of a dream job, to work in the world of civil rights." Although she was proud to have the job, after three years Adrienne felt she was not going to be intellectually challenged. She also felt her career choices were part of the debate in the seventies about personal change versus social change. Since she and many of her friends were benefiting by personal psychotherapy, she decided to get therapy training, thus starting another phase of her career.

Adrienne was turned down by six out of the seven therapy training programs to which she applied. They argued that her experiences would be different from other people's and that her clients might feel too sorry for her to talk about themselves. She sued the program that had been her top choice, and in an out-of-court settlement they agreed to admit her. She wonders if she was wrong in not going to the place that accepted her. Her life was made difficult in her program by the hostile attitude she encountered, stemming from, she believes, their anger about the lawsuit. When Adrienne applied to the therapy programs, she also applied to graduate schools for a Ph.D. "I figured if I got a Ph.D., I'd have more leverage [getting therapy training]." She got into a program in social psychology at Columbia where she wanted to study the relationship between personality and politics. Because her therapy program was scheduled mostly at night, she decided she could do both. "I was crazy!" Adrienne notes. Furthermore, she was still doing some civil rights counseling to make money. Eventually, her personal life began falling apart. Two important serious relationships broke up—one with a man she had lived with for seven years—and several close friends moved from New York.

"The consequence was that I didn't do well," Adrienne says. "I was dysfunctional. I was miserable—trying to do [more than] two things at once. I was really quite a basket case!" But she kept going and eventually finished both programs—the therapy program in 1981 and her Ph.D. much later, in 1992.

Another turning point in Adrienne's career and intellectual interests came about through a friendship with a fellow graduate student at Columbia. Michelle Fine, who was, Adrienne says, "destined to be an academic superstar," asked Adrienne to collaborate with her on a journal article about the double discrimination of women with disabilities. Adrienne agreed to collaborate on the article if they could ask the question, "Is there really double discrimination?" and if they would not assume the answer beforehand. The article, "Disabled Women: Sexism without the Pedestal," was a great success and led to duo talks at conferences and a request in 1982 for Adrienne to design a course at Barnard on the disabled person in American society. She had never taught before and there were no models for such a course, but Adrienne says, "I had the right instinct about how to make a course that looked at disability from a lot of complex viewpoints." She found that she loved teaching.

At the same time, because she had run out of money, Adrienne had gone back to her old job at the New York State Division of Human Rights and was still counseling some patients in therapy. She was also trying to work on her Ph.D. dissertation. However, her next step in her career interests came as a by-product of developing the new course on disability. Adrienne describes her introduction to that field.

In looking for an intellectual framework to use for her course, Adrienne discovered bioethics, which was to become her major interest in research and teaching. As she was planning her course, someone suggested that Adrienne meet with a professor of bioethics at Columbia. When she discussed some of the questions in disability policy that interested her, he immediately referred her to a bioethics reader in which she found many of the issues addressed, particularly about how much of society's resources should be allocated to health care. She immediately saw the analogy between that question and how much of society's resources should become accessible to the disabled. However, she disagreed with the attitudes in bioethics articles about life with disabilities. She began to go to bioethics meetings where the latest national cases were being discussed—the Jane Doe case, for example, involving the parents' right to refuse treatment for their infant with spina bifida, and another, the Elizabeth Bouvia case, where Bouvia, who had cerebral palsy, wanted to be allowed to starve herself to death. Adrienne felt the participants in the discussions were "missing some things," as she says. At the New York State Bar Association Conference in May 1984, where cases of infants who would have disabilities or handicaps were being discussed, she spoke up. She describes the experience:

I wore my best suit and went to the meeting so I could listen from the audience. There were four talks. Two of them were good; two of them were awful. And then it was time for questions and I was recognized, although I don't know how. I mean, "The blind woman in the back?" They didn't know my name or anything. But anyway, I said, "This is all very interesting, and some of these talks have been very good, but you have never heard from anybody with a disability about what it means to live with a disability. And if you had, maybe you wouldn't think living with spina bifida was such a bad thing." Then I sat down.

Adrienne's comments at that meeting led ultimately to her involvement in the field of bioethics. After the talks she met several people who encouraged her input and invited her to other conferences. She says, "I totally fell in love with the field—fell in love with the people, fell in love with the field." Meanwhile, in 1984, after she had published two articles about disability in a major psychology journal, her interests suddenly began to cohere. She attended a three-day conference on disability in Wisconsin, which she describes as "the most important intellectual experience as a conference on disability that I'd ever been at because it had disability scholars, disability activists, and the head of the ACLU, which had been on the wrong side of disability issues up to this time."

Personally and professionally, Adrienne could see how her commitments to civil rights and bioethics could come together and be used. She expanded her work from just disability to other issues, including questions of reproduction. By 1985 she was able to stop working at the New York State Division of Human Rights to concentrate on her graduate work. However, her active involvement in her new discipline and in teaching and research kept her from completing all her doctoral requirements. She says, "People would ask me to write this paper or do that conference or edit this book or teach some other thing, and I kept saying yes. I [discovered] how much I liked doing them."

In 1987 Adrienne became a full-time staff person for the newly created New Jersey Bioethics Commission and stayed there for three years. Her book with Michelle Fine, *Women with Disabilities*, was published in 1988 and was very well regarded. For two years she did consulting and freelance work and continued to work on her dissertation. "I sort of created niches for myself," she says, "and I had become knowledgeable about things I had never studied." In 1992, Adrienne left New York to take a job at Boston University's School of Social Work for two years and then got her "dream job," as Henry R. Luce Professor of Biology, Ethics, and the Politics of Human Reproduction at Wellesley College. Adrienne describes her work as "spectacularly satisfying." She adds, "I love going to work every day."

Sometime after our interview I discussed Adrienne's narrative with her. She said she would like to further explain her love of her work and teaching, and she sent me something in writing:

> I love this job because I love the variety of courses I teach here and the many roles I play at this institution. I am still excited about the courses I teach after nine years, and I am always trying to make them better, to make my teaching better.
>
> I have enjoyed the diversity of my work: collaboration with other faculty on projects, service on college committees, direction of independent study projects, which include subjects such as reproductive rights of women on public assistance, commercial surrogate motherhood, doctor-patient relationships in Greece, social services to Korean elderly in Atlanta, and many more.
>
> Sometimes disability issues are part of my courses; at other times, there is nothing particular about disability in them. I can champion disability issues when necessary, but that is not my role and not the principal way I am perceived here. I love that I have the chance to be liked or disliked, respected or not, for my ability to teach, my ability to collaborate with others, and to be a mentor to all kinds of students.
>
> Some of my happiest moments have come from the fact that students of mine have invited me to their weddings, have celebrated with me when they got into medical school, have wanted to stay in touch with me and keep me in their lives. A student in one of the many course evaluations one gets at the end of a semester wrote: "I want to be Adrienne." She certainly wasn't saying she wanted to be the sometimes disorganized, sometimes frantic person who is blind; but she saw something in who I was and what I did that inspired her and that respect and regard means a lot to me—more than I can say.

Adrienne did not want to conclude her interview without acknowledging that work is not all of life. She says, "Although I have never married and raised my own children, I have had deep relationships, wonderful friendships, and the joy of being close to the children of several friends. At a women's college, with all my women friends there is a lot of discussion about "balancing" work and life—especially life as a mother. I haven't faced the work-and-children struggle, but I constantly wrestle with how to maintain a nonwork life with room for friendship, love, political commitments, involvement in choral and chamber music, and just fun.

"I can't say that either being a woman or being blind makes that juggling act worse for me than anyone else; I can say that it is hard to do, and I'm not always sure I have the balance I would like."

She concludes, "Blindness is something I have to factor into my life, just the same way that someone with a two-hour commute to work or with complicated child care arrangements needs to factor that into their life. Blindness is not the challenge; the challenge is the attitudes that people have toward blindness and disability, and the consequent struggle with public discrimination and personal dismissal and stereotyping. Those odds are mostly socially created and are largely socially changeable."

SALLY

"When I ended up in a wheelchair, I knew absolutely that I had to change my image."

I met Sally through a mutual friend at a Christmas party. A sixty-one-year old food technologist, she had polio at fifteen and for much of her life showed little signs of her disability. However, she was in a wheelchair when we met, and she also skillfully maneuvered an electric scooter when I saw her later at a meeting of the Greater Boston Post Polio Association. She had retired five years previously and had loved her work in food research. For the interview I went to her house, where she served me a delicious lunch and showed me around her place, which is well adapted to her limited walking ability.

Sally contracted polio in the summer of 1952 at the start of a vacation with her parents and four brothers. On the first day in the motel where they were staying, she developed a severe headache and then found that she could not move her limbs. She was hospitalized for three months, paralyzed from the neck down, and was briefly on a chest respirator. She remembers the feeling of panic she experienced when she was removed from the ventilator—initially only five minutes the first day.

Right from the start, her parents faced her illness with determination and optimism. Her father, Sally says, was "a challenger and enforcer" whose philosophy was "fear nothing but fear itself." Her mother, who had contracted and recovered from polio eighteen months after her marriage, brought her coloring books in the hospital, knowing that Sally could only use her hands. The major turning point in her rehabilitation was a seven-month stay at the Georgia Warm Springs Foundation, founded in 1927 by President Franklin Delano Roosevelt for the rehabilitation of polio patients. Sally recalls that she arrived at Warm Springs at Halloween on a stretcher and left in May, walking out the front gate using crutches and two long leg braces, which she was later able to abandon. She remembers her time at Warm Springs fondly, almost tearfully, as she recalls the fun of teenage gatherings and events. She also took courses to keep up with her sophomore high school class, and she was able, with some extra tutoring after she returned home to Louisville, Kentucky, to graduate with her class at the private Catholic high school she attended.

Sally was encouraged to go to college, particularly by her father. She considered leaving Louisville to attend college and study chemistry, but when she was offered a four-year scholarship in dietetics at Ursuline College in Louisville, she decided to accept the offer. There she earned a B.A. in chemistry and dietetics. One of the nuns, later to become president of the college, was her special mentor and encouraged her to go on to graduate school. In 1961 Sally received her M.A. from Iowa State University, having won a two-year assistantship in food research.

She returned to Louisville to look for work, partly, she says, because "I was dating a couple of guys I liked in the area." She found a job as a technician in a medical school, doing biomedical research. It paid "a pittance" and after two and a half years, Sally realized the job was a dead end and that she had to make a decision to get an advanced degree—probably a Ph.D. in chemistry—or look for a job in her field of food research. She decided on the latter.

Sally's connection with New England and the Boston area had begun earlier when she had given a college research paper at Suffolk University and discovered Bailey's hot fudge ice cream sundaes. In 1962 she was maid of honor at a friend's wedding in Connecticut and met a young man who, as she says, "became attached to me."

"He called me every day and came to visit me for all the big holidays in Kentucky. We began thinking about being really serious." In December 1963, she went to Connecticut to meet his family and also contacted the food research lab in the Boston area about a job she had applied for earlier. She immediately got an appointment.

"She [the employer] set up a date on the twenty-eighth of December. It was exactly that date. I borrowed my friend's car and drove up and I had my interview. They hired me on the spot."

Sally thought she'd probably stay at the job a couple of years. Her boss warned her that the town where the lab was located would not be very exciting for a young person. "But," Sally says, "I was willing to give it a shot." That was 1963 and she stayed until 1993. "I guess I stayed a few years longer," she says.

For many years, Sally's disability was not a factor in her work life. Occasionally she used a cane, and once after a fall, she was on crutches for a while. In our interview, she emphasized that her work experience was not much related to her disability. However, she did describe important times when it was an issue, noting that it became important after a disastrous operation in July 1983 when she was forty-six years old and was operated on to correct a curvature of the spine. Unfortunately, her mobility was severely damaged by the operation. The surgery was elective, and Sally says, "[It was] the worst mistake in my life." She was in pulmonary intensive care for three weeks after the operation. Fortunately, she had insisted on a hospital with that kind of expertise because her regular doctor had warned her that she might experience pulmonary trouble—not uncommon for polio patients after anesthesia. However, the disaster was from the surgery, which resulted in her never being able to stand independently again. After the operation, the surgeon had said simply, "I'm sorry," but he offered no explanation of what had happened. Sally commented that she knew she could—and perhaps should—have sued for malpractice, but she didn't really believe in suing.

"The operation didn't stop my work," Sally says. "I worked from my hospital bed. I never lost pace. I never lost any pay."

The failed operation did have a significant effect on Sally's life and her work experience. She struggled for two years to use crutches and found it too wearing. She says, "I had no arm strength. I would drag myself home, and fortunately we had food during the day because I was doing recipe developments and that's what I ate. I would come home and go straight to bed. That's all the strength I had." She bought a wheelchair and had someone at the labs help her from her car. She would call from the gate to tell someone to meet her with the wheelchair and then, at the end of the day, find someone to take her to her car. Finally she bought three wheelchairs—one for her car, one at home, and one at work. Eventually she purchased a van and a scooter, which gave her a great deal more mobility. Most of this equipment came at her own expense.

I asked Sally if using a wheelchair made a difference in attitudes toward her at work. She recalled that there was a change. She felt she had to constantly prove her professionalism. She says, "They would think you could not make a presentation because you were in a wheelchair." She mimics, " 'My goodness, how would that look? A person in a wheelchair giving a presentation!' "

She continues, "There's an initial reaction which is negative which you have to overcome." She recalls that she was selected by the Kaiser Foundation to present at a conference of food professionals at Palo Alto, California. "I was chosen," she says, "because I was considered the major authority in this country for developing quantity recipes that were low fat." She went to her boss to get permission to go, and he said, "What would happen if you were run over by a truck?" "Meaning," Sally says, "did I really need to go?"

Sally added that the same man had used the same question—"What would happen if you were run over by a truck?"—eight years before when she was temporarily on crutches and had asked permission to accept an invitation to give an important paper at the Institute of Food Technology's annual meeting. We agreed that her boss was at best inarticulate and at worst discriminatory.

In addition to her employer's discriminatory attitude toward her disability, Sally's perception of herself also changed. She says, "You know, after I ended up in a wheelchair, I was faced with the reality that I was disabled. Before that, it just had never crossed my mind." She explains, "I knew absolutely that I had to change my image. When I used to go to work I wasn't required to look like I was highly successful—you know, to wear expensive suits and dresses. But when I was in a wheelchair, I made a decision. I was going to dress for success because I realized that people thought that if you were in a wheelchair, you were really not as professionally competent as someone who wasn't in a chair. I know that. Absolutely. I still know that now. So, I totally changed my image."

Although Sally acknowledged that her disability had affected her work environment and even her attitude toward herself, she never allowed it to adversely affect the quality of her work. She also spoke about another kind of discrimination, that of gender—of prejudiced attitudes toward women that she felt were ingrained in the culture of her workplace in the "old boy network," as she described it.

"There is an issue for women in the workplace," she says, "There is no question." She explained that in her workplace, at the labs, fewer women than men reached the higher government grade levels. In fact, for many years no women reached the higher level of grade 13, although her boss, a woman, finally reached that level at her retirement.

"As a woman," Sally commented, "you really have to do more than anybody else would do. There's no question of that. In addition to that, you'd better be assertive. Because if you aren't, if you don't get out there and let your light glow, or let everybody become aware of your accomplishments, then it [advancement] is not going to happen."

When I asked her if there was anything, looking back, that she would have changed in her own attitude to her work, she says, "Absolutely. I would be far more assertive. I see that the squeaky wheel gets the grease. My major fault when I worked was I always thought if I did a good job or an outstanding job, which after all I did, I would be recognized. But that's not the case."

By way of illustrating her point, Sally described the process she went through trying to raise her employment grade to 12. She recalled how her director called her in to explain why one of her colleagues was being raised to grade 12 and Sally was staying at grade 11: "He said, 'The reason I have to make her a 12 and not you is because she has been making so much noise at the personnel office that we have to do this. I really think it should be you, but feel assured you will be getting yours shortly.'"

It was nine years before Sally got the higher grade. Meanwhile, about five years later, when her immediate boss attended the funeral of Sally's father, she told her mother Sally was about to get a raise. Again, nothing happened. Finally, after a personnel fight within her division when Sally mobilized and made the case for a colleague, her scientific director, she was rewarded by him at his retirement with a raise to grade level 12. It had all taken nine years and only after she had become assertive on behalf of someone else!

Recognizing that her disability as well as her position as a disabled woman influenced her work life, Sally became an advocate for the disabled. "I got involved in the Disability Committee at work. One of the deputy commanders at the labs had a child with a disability. "He fought for us," she says. "You have to have somebody fighting."

At fifty-five, Sally decided to retire. She realized she would always overextend herself. She often worked ten to eleven hours a day. She says, "I'm not the kind of person that can deliver the minimum amount. I have always done my share and somebody else's. It's just part of my family ethics. We're all workaholics."

She adds, "There was a lot of stress. I don't deny that. The last six months I worked it was often difficult to find the strength to push my wheelchair." When she heard, almost by chance from a colleague, that they were offering a $25,000 incentive for retirement for anyone who had a certain minimum age and amount of time accumulated, she decided to apply.

The next morning at 7:00 A.M. Sally was at her office, putting together her documentation for the personnel department. The offer was limited to the first forty people who applied and were eligible.

At first her boss didn't believe Sally. He said, "Come on, you're not old enough!" and then, "You don't have enough years either." He didn't take her seriously until she sent over her paperwork and kept reminding him of her decision. "Finally, he got the message," Sally says.

That was March. Sally continues, "I wasn't eligible to retire until December, but believe me, as soon as that day came, I was out the door! I could have enjoyed staying longer, but it was very difficult for me to work [by then]."

In our follow-up interview, Sally reflected that although many of her decisions about her career did not relate to her disability, it had impacted her work life; her decision to retire at fifty-five was mostly because of her physical condition. She feels she has been adventurous and has trusted her own sense of what she can do. She has traveled, extensively in this country and some internationally. She enjoyed her work, she says, but feels she did not get much recognition for what she did.

At present Sally is active in advocacy for the disabled. Her major interest has been in making Boston important as a ventilator center (a ventilator is an assistive device often needed by post-polio patients). She has also advocated for more accessibility in restaurants, churches, and other institutions, and she's been a member of the Disability Policy Consortium that meets at the state house. I remember that the day I first interviewed Sally, she spoke on the phone to someone and afterward said she wanted to organize a group of volunteers to keep in touch with people who were homebound and needed to talk with someone in their daily lives. It seems that Sally, like many of the women I interviewed, has taken on another career of advocacy in her life.

KRISTEN

"I just really think if you have a visible disability, you're not going to get a job."

risten and I arranged to meet in the Emmanuel College cafeteria. She arrived with her husband, Kevin, who had driven their van to work at the public health research project where they were employed part-time. Kristen had polio as a one-year-old and has used an electric wheelchair for many years. She has some impairment in one arm, which slows but does not impede her eating dexterity. We found a table but unfortunately couldn't escape a lot of the cafeteria's noise. Despite that, we managed to have a good conversation. Some time later I called Kristen to ask her some questions we didn't have time to cover.

Born in 1951 and stricken with polio in 1952, Kristen says she was more sheltered than her three brothers and one sister, but that it was expected that she would do everything she was able to do. "My mother did it all," she says, referring to her mother's dominant role. However, her mother kept a tight rein on Kristen, particularly when it involved a boyfriend. Probably because of that, Kristen left home in her late twenties to go live with her boyfriend and two years later, she had a child. She returned home briefly when her daughter was about three and a half but found family relationships too difficult for her to stay.

Kristen attended a school for the disabled until ninth grade, where she learned about being with others who were disabled and about the hierarchy that exists among the disabled in an institutional community. Those who could walk, she says, with or without crutches (often polio survivors), were ranked at the top of the status scale. In contrast, the wheelchair users were placed somewhere near the bottom of the scale. During those years she had a spinal fusion and still contends with problems from a curvature of the spine.

Kristen does not remember overt discrimination about her disability in the public high school she attended. "I didn't feel different," she says, but she was not able to use the bathroom all day because they were not accessible. She had a few girlfriends, who helped her navigate her manual wheelchair, but she didn't have much to do with boys, she says, although her friends wanted to set her up with a boy with a spinal cord injury who used a wheelchair. Her reaction was negative, she admits, and remembers that she kept complaining, "What am I going to do with Harry?" Years later, she met him again and they were friendly even though she confessed to him, "I hated you all through high school."

She is not sure whether her guidance counselor suggested that she go into secretarial work because she was a woman or because she was disabled, but after high school graduation, she attended a two-year commercial college—essentially a secretarial school. After she completed the program and began to look for a job, she began a series of frustrating experiences with the state rehabilitation services. She explains: "I didn't have an electric wheelchair, so I couldn't get around very well. But when I went [to rehab] to request a wheelchair, they said I had to have a job before I [could get] a wheelchair!"

Because of the catch-22 transportation situation and her lack of success in getting a job, Kristen decided to continue her education, first at a community college, where she completed a liberal arts program, and then a four-year college. In her educational experiences, Kristen found that her poor training in math and science kept her out of her preferred major, psychology. However, with perseverance, she did graduate with a B.A. in English in 1980. Ironically, as long as she was a student, her subsidized transportation was provided by state services, but when she became employed, she was on her own.

Kristen was still living at home when she got her first job in an independent living center, to which her family provided the transportation. After a year of work, she felt she had to live her own life, and in her late twenties she left home to move in with her boyfriend. Getting to and from work became impossible since they did not own a car (nor could she drive) and she was using a wheelchair—although by now she had an electric one.

Kristen challenges the stereotype that disabled women are unable to have and raise children. Her daughter was born in 1982. She describes her pregnancy as "wonderful," and despite the doctor's warnings that she might have to stay in bed the last three months of her pregnancy, she remained healthy and active. The delivery by cesarean was not as easy because she was given a paralyzing agent that spread to her lungs and landed her in intensive care. Fortunately, she recovered rapidly.

Kristen says her daughter's father was enthusiastic about having a child, insisting he had wanted to have a baby "since he was twelve years old." He became the child's primary caretaker for a year and a half but then, as Kristen put it, "he wanted out" and left them. She still remembers her daughter, as she grew up, saying, "Ma, you know how you told me my father would stop by? How come he hasn't?"

Kristen did not look for work at that time because she wanted to stay home to be with her daughter for a while and care for her. She says, "I didn't really try to work after she was born because I wanted to get her to a certain point where I wouldn't have to leave her with strangers." She explained that the daily personal care assistants that she has for her own needs (provided by Medicaid through her father's health insurance) were able to help her with the baby. However, at one point she did take in a sixteen-year-old girl from New Jersey, whose ad in the paper offering child care stated that she was eighteen. Apparently, the girl wanted to get away from home, and although her step-mother saw the ad, she sent her away anyway. Kristen, whom the girl called "Mumsie," says, "She learned to do things real early." The arrangement didn't last very long.

Kristen's husband, Kevin, came into the picture when her daughter was three and a half and has taken on a father's role since then. (Rebecca, her daughter, was sixteen when I conducted this interview.) A major issue for Kristen and Kevin as a family is that they cannot get legally married because if they do, Kristen will lose all of her benefits, including her personal care assistants. As Kristen says, "We are married in the eyes of the church, but not by the state," and that is for them "the biggest problem."

We talked about children of disabled mothers and whether they ever expressed their feelings about being in that position. Kristen says her daughter has never really discussed her disability with her. She says, "I haven't actually ever asked her. I never saw it bother her, but maybe [underneath] it may bother her. She's acted out—a little too much in the past. I have a friend whose mother said to me [once] that she thinks my daughter is bitter because I'm disabled. Where did she get that? I don't really think that."

Kristen admits that at times she worried that Rebecca would not have friends "because she had a mother in a wheelchair." However, she has found that has not been the case. "[Rebecca's] friends," she says, "are not like that at all, and they have never been. Never, ever."

Furthermore, occasionally her daughter has surprised her with her comments and insights. She recalls that once when her daughter was eleven, Kristen was telling her the story of two friends who had been in an accident and had received spinal cord injuries and how depressed and sad she felt for them. She remembers her daughter lying across the bed, wide-eyed as she spoke, but when she finished the story, her daughter said, "Mom, you crack me up! You told me that story like *you* are not even in a wheelchair!"

She also remarks that her daughter hardly seems to notice that a person is disabled. She says once when a friend, who uses a wheelchair, came to visit, her daughter commented when he had gone, "I never noticed that Henry was disabled." When Kristen asked, "So what did you think, Henry was just lazy, rolling around in the wheelchair because he felt like it?" Rebecca insisted, "No, but I just never noticed."

In the 1990s Kristen returned to college to do graduate work and received her master's degree as a rehabilitation counselor. Her experience at the university was not good, she says, mostly because of the problem of transportation to the campus in Boston. She was eligible to take The Ride, the notoriously ineffective MBTA (Massachusetts Bay Transportation Authority) public transportation system for the disabled and elderly, but, she says, "it was awful." She explains, "I had to take The Ride at least two hours ahead of what I needed, change to another Ride and go to the campus, where I waited for hours and got home at 9:00 P.M." She was ready to quit, but her husband insisted she hang on and ended up driving her back and forth for the last four semesters in their late model van.

She also had to fight hard to get the state rehabilitation services to pay for her graduate work, although they regularly subsidize M.A.'s and even Ph.D.'s. They had told her when her child was born that she was reclassified as a homemaker and that her case was closed as far as the agency was concerned. She finally qualified for support but had to take out a $7,500 loan to get started. When she was awarded a cash prize of $2,500 from a university fund, she says, "I never received the money. I never even received a notice [from the rehab agency] that I won the award." They simply took the money. Despite the struggle, Kristen received her M.A. in rehabilitation counseling in 1996.

During her graduate work, Kristen had an internship at a rehabilitation hospital, but she evaluates the internship as a mixed experience. Although she feels the hospital is a good one for patients, she felt the internship program was not well run. Her supervisor did not give her opportunities in the whole spectrum of counseling and would assign her to do five-minute summaries from new patients whom she would never see again. She never had the chance to follow through their cases. Kristen felt that because she was in a wheelchair, the supervisor limited her. After complaining to her university adviser, he interviewed the supervisor and she subsequently received better assignments.

Kristen feels that "you can advocate for someone else better than you can for yourself," and she would like to be a patient advocate in a hospital. In particular, she would like to help patients make the transition to the disabled world. She says, "I want to be the piece of the puzzle that helps somebody who was able-bodied but injured [make] a transition to the disabled world. [I want to be] the person who goes in and sits and talks to them, slowly working them [through the transition]."

When I asked if there was anyone who did that kind of work now, she says, "In Massachusetts there is no such animal." She explains that the social worker doesn't do it because she doesn't have time, and the rehab counselor is trying to get patients either back to school or back to work.

Kristen particularly admires her friends with spinal cord injuries because she feels they are far more aggressive than people who have been disabled all of their lives. They remember their life before the injury and are less willing to accept the disabled status. Kristen sums up their attitude toward the world: "If I did that last year, damn it, I'm going to do it this year and you're going to fix it so I can."

Kristen has learned that if you are disabled, you need some of that attitude to get the world to let you be part of it. She also feels, like many others I spoke to, that the rehabilitation counseling is not adequate, but also that the world of employment is not open to hiring or accommodating the disabled, particularly those in wheelchairs. She says, "Even McDonalds won't hire you if you go there in a wheelchair. When you think of it, what can you do? You can't even reach the cash register. Lots of disabled people in wheelchairs could cashier, but they can't reach the cash register. Try to tell a store that! Wal-Mart put welfare mothers to work. Well, why not put disabled people to work? Lower your cash registers and give people a place to go to work!"

Although Kristen and her husband were working as research assistants for a project on disability at a university at the time of the interview, unfortunately the project ended because of the untimely death of the director. Kristen is not optimistic about work opportunities for the disabled. She sums up her experience when she says, "I just really think that if you have a visible disability, you're not going to get a job. Even now with the ADA [Americans with Disabilities Act]—who enforces it? We need police for the ADA," she concludes.

When I asked Kristen where she would rate work in importance in her life, she says, near the top, right after family. Presently, however, she is not seeking work because she is experiencing recurring medical problems, particularly due to the spinal curvature. She does, however, feel good about her family life and her success in raising her daughter, who wants to be a nurse practitioner and is working at a medical clinic.

JUDITH

"We need a new definition of work."

interviewed Judith in her modest town house where she has lived for many years. A soft-spoken but intense fifty-six-year-old woman, she led me to the table in the dining area and cleared papers and magazines so that we could set up the tape recorder. Like Carol in part 2, Judith appears to be an able-bodied person but has invisible disabilities. As a young adult, she developed multiple chemical sensitivities where exposure to certain foods, solvents, and pollutants triggers physical, emotional, and psychological symptoms and dissociative disorders including arthritis, bursitis, Crohn's disease, kidney insufficiency, bipolar syndrome, and chronic fatigue syndrome. She explained in her interview that as her symptoms developed, she was not able to work regularly in a full-time job and therefore had to find her own way of being productive. Recently, Judith provided some additional comments to questions I posed, which I have included in the narrative.

Judith's story, like those in part 1, is partly about how her disabilities developed and how she learned to think of disability as part of her identity and as a condition that she could frame for herself. Her account also focuses on her discovery of how work could be part of her life and how she has come to understand a broader definition of work, particularly for the disabled.

Although Judith says that in her school years through high school, her disabilities were not apparent, she remembers that in childhood, her emotional and sensory sensitivities were acute. She says, "I had a constitution that is hard to explain. The least little touch was painful to me as a young child, and I didn't have any way of defending [myself] from that." She continues, "When I was seven or eight I was fitted with sunglasses and given some kind of daily medicine. The thought was that I was allergic to the sun. I got poison ivy even without contacting it, just from the oils in the air."

Recently Judith was given a medical hypothesis that suggests that her body is unable to perform a particular liver metabolic function that impacts her ability to deal with toxins. She comments, "Meanwhile the toxins in our environment are on the increase. And the impact is cumulative. More and more people are showing signs of toxicity because of the world we live in." Judith has explored the area of her supersensitivity and her attempt to find "a good boundary in proximity" in her book, published in 1999, *More Than Meets the Eye: Energy.*

After graduating from high school in 1961, Judith went to Antioch College but soon after had a nervous breakdown that kept her from continuing her education for several years. She worked at different jobs and started college again in 1965 at Boston University. Meanwhile, she had fallen in love and moved in with the man who became her husband. She says, "[My father, who had paid for my education] said he couldn't continue to support me if I was going to share my living quarters with a man, so of course, the choice I made was no school." (Her father died in 1968.) Judith married and had a daughter, but the marriage ended in divorce.

I asked Judith if her daughter shares her life. She says that her daughter, who has since moved to Oregon, "keeps her distance." She adds, "She doesn't communicate with me much. And it's probably just as well." She explains, "Even when she was here and in high school she moved from the second bedroom down into the basement. She experienced the other side of a lot of what I've been through. In her childhood, my first hospitalization for manic depression was when she was six. Now she works as a special education teacher with adolescents who are emotionally disturbed." She added, "We're very close but at a distance. Which is good for me and very good for her."

Judith did not get back to her education after her marriage and divorce, but she found a job at a research company, which gave her a sense of purpose and satisfaction. She says, "I had been sent there for a three-day typing assignment and ended up there for seventeen years. It was like being in a graduate school with constant learning." Unfortunately, as her health deteriorated, Judith began to miss days of work. Eventually, she was told to leave and to go on disability. This came as a real shock to her. She says, "It was like cutting off a limb or cutting out my heart." She explains, "I needed so much approval, and I used work as a way to get it. It was very devastating to lose my way of reaching out to people."

Despite discouraging advice from a state rehabilitation counselor, who told her she would never work because of her limitations, Judith found part-time work. She was employed at the Fernald School, one day a week, in vocational services with people who had severe cognitive dysfunctions. Over five years, she helped clients express their needs and desires to live independently, taking the approach that their disabilities should not be defined as fixed clinical conditions but rather as part of their identity as individuals who can contribute to society and who need to build self-esteem. This experience helped her develop her ideas about disability and her interest in helping others to refocus their lives. She would eventually think of herself as the "wounded healer."

Meanwhile, through her work on a research project on work and disability, Judith met someone who was an important influence in her thinking about disability and life. Moro Fleming, director of consumer involvement at the state rehabilitation commission, contacted her about his being a volunteer in the research project. He had developed epilepsy from a brain tumor and was interested in the study. Although she was ready for their relationship to be adversarial because of her negative experience with the state rehabilitation counselor, she found that they shared a similar vision. Judith recalls their first conversation.

"I had the most amazing conversation with him," she says. "It went on for two hours. We just fed each other, and that was the beginning of an incredible relationship." She continues, "We shared a spiritual connection and a large sweeping lens, which gave a unique perspective on disability." She adds, "[We shared] a vision not simply focused on disability but a vision about the way the world could be if informed by a natural idealism and a sense of connection."

She concludes, "He later died of that brain tumor in 1990. It was very hard. I get shivers when I think about it because I think that he's still a part of me. He was a very spiritual person. Meeting him was a pivotal point in my life."

Judith became involved in the commission's plans and work. Fleming hired her at first to do small jobs like stuffing envelopes for mailings, but then he asked her to attend advisory committee meetings. She explains, "At first, I was ex officio. I would just go and listen and could not vote. Then I was invited to be part of it. It went on for a long time—eight years." She feels her relationship with the advisory committee was very satisfying. Some of her ideas got translated into everyday practices.

"I learned a lot and learned how at the top the vision is there," she recalls. "But there's a big gap. How do you bring the vision down to the day-to-day activities? It's a big issue in our world." She recalls that at the Fernald School she saw the same problem: "At Fernald, they'd issue these orders and they'd have no idea how impossible it was to put what they were saying into effect. They never came down from the castle." She continues, "I used to think it should be required that everyone in administrative positions should work a week every six months in direct care. Similarly, those people [in direct care] need to come to the administrative offices. People get attached to a role and are not able to see other points of view."

Among the projects that Judith developed at the rehab commission was a consumer registry—a list of the clients' skills that could be used at the agency. There are, she says, well over 100 consumer consultants on the list who have been hired, including herself. She had just been on a team that did a study to find out the work status of 606 people who during 1991 to 1992 had completed services from the agency. The study investigated "why so few persons who are receiving SSDI [social security disability insurance] return to gainful full-time work and even fewer relinquish benefits."[5]

Judith summarized the most valuable information she felt they uncovered in the study: "Eighty-five percent of the people said that what kept them from working was their disability. It tells me how inadequate the medical model is. Disability keeps people from working because the stakes are so high. If you work, you'll lose your benefits. You don't trust yourself or the world to support you. If you're afraid that if you recover, you'll lose everything, how are you going to recover?" In other words, she suggests, disabled people are afraid of losing not only their benefits but also their identity as disabled. They get attached to that identity and defined by it. That, she believes, must change. She continues, "The whole disability system is built on fixity. Right now a person's social security benefit is based upon their proving what they can't do. And the rehab commission can only get funding for people if it stays in the state and federal [medical] paradigm of disability."

Judith has also been a tutor for the agency, helping people acclimate to the workplace. She explains her particular approach, which is consistent with her philosophy about disability: "The real value I can offer people is in the realm of emotional release and stress management, helping them get out of their own way. We all get these weird opinions about ourselves, but the worst are the ones that are internalized." She concludes, "Whether people have a disability or not, we're all limited and disabled by our own mental and psychic material, and I think we are here in order to work with it."

Judith has started a healing and fitness business. She also teaches tai chi. Her healing practices and philosophy have developed over the years from her reading in spirituality and philosophy and from her own experiences. She explains, "At the heart of most spiritual teaching is a shift of focus. It requires that we be willing to give up a narrative, and calling ourselves disabled may be part of that narrative that we have to be willing to give up. Disability is a social construct. We have many choices, and among them is how to frame our experiences. That in fact is probably the most powerful choice we can make."

Judith's second academic experience was very positive. She received a degree in psychology of health and illness in 1988 from Lesley College, where she found her interests and experience could be used in her studies. She is currently studying for a master's degree in interdisciplinary inquiry, where she will continue to use her own experience as part of her research into illness identity. She explains, "I have a very quick mind, but the hardest thing for me is that my intellect is emotionally based."

Judith commented that she has lived a "shamanic life" and that she had to learn to live "in a shamanic body." I asked her if she could say more about what she meant by the shamanic life. Judith explains, "I think the degree of sensitivity I have, the extent to which I am psychic or empathic or intuitive, the degree to which I constantly receive and transmit information from other dimensions—these are all characteristics of a shaman."

She continues, "In another culture, they [these characteristics] would be recognized and cultivated from infancy. There would be a special role for someone with a constitution like my own. I'd have a position in the community as a healer. But we aren't living in that kind of world."

"I've had to devote myself to discovering ways to make it work," she concludes, "and then I've been able to share what I've learned through my books, my teaching, and [my] clients. That has been a great gift."

Elaborating on the subject of work, Judith explains that she could not be locked into a job where she had to report in daily and keep to a rigid schedule. She receives support from SSDI. The kind of teaching and counseling that she does now, however, she says, "helps me use all of who I am."

Her experience and coming to understand her own disabilities and her unique gifts give her insight into others' limitations. She says, "I am witnessing that more people than ever are beginning to share the challenges I have been facing all of my life. It is gratifying to be able to be of some help to these individuals."

She has also formed a conviction that we need a new definition of work. She has described it this way: "Work does not have to mean finding a job that fits into an already defined system which might have no room for a person who is innovative or whose needs and abilities are not standard. Work means having a productive role to play in the world. Start with the assets. We can invent jobs that meet a real external need and capitalize on a person's talents and skills. There is a myth that only the self-employed are entrepreneurs. But today, in order to survive, all employees need to be entrepreneurs. Everything is in the framing, the reframing."

ALICIA

"Find your own life work."

licia came to my office at Emmanuel College for her interview. Born with cerebral palsy, she is a striking, dark-haired young woman who could easily be mistaken for someone in her twenties, not thirty-seven years old. She uses a crutch to help balance her in walking, and her speech is a little difficult to understand at first. However, despite her soft-spoken voice, I was soon able to understand her conversation. Unfortunately, the tape recorder did not pick up her speech clearly, so I was unable to fully quote her often insightful comments. I contacted her again later to update her story.

Alicia was born in Portugal and moved to this country in 1972 when she was ten. The family lived in Somerville, Massachusetts. She has a younger brother with whom she is very close. "We are very supportive of each other," she says. She gives her whole family much credit for being supportive of her as a disabled person. She adds, "Perhaps [they were] too protective." At twenty-five she decided to leave home so she could become more independent, realizing that her family had to adapt not only to having a disabled child but also to having a daughter who had different expectations from the typical girl in "old–world Portugal." Alicia wanted a career in art, a notion that seemed at first inappropriate to her parents but to which they adjusted. Now they are very pleased. She says, "I think I have changed them a lot."

Her first educational experience was a public school, which she found very difficult because of her disability. Her family decided to send her to the Cotting School, a chapter 766 (publicly financed) private day school in Lexington, Massachusetts, for girls and boys with physical, communication, and learning disabilities. Alicia says her experience there was very good. Like several other women in this project who attended a special school for the disabled, she felt the school taught her a lot about her disability and made her feel comfortable with it. However, she also felt the teachers did not push students enough with an academic curriculum that would better prepare them to go on to higher education.

After graduating in 1982 at twenty-one, she was encouraged by her guidance counselors to go to Bunker Hill Community College where she studied human services and was financially supported by the state rehabilitation agency and federal grants. I asked Alicia if she wished that she had chosen another concentration in college, since she eventually chose to go to art school. "I thought I was interested in working with children," she says, and she concludes that she didn't really know what she wanted to do at that point.

Alicia graduated from Bunker Hill in 1985. Her peers in college were all taking jobs. "That's what you were expected to do," she says, and so she started to work at the children's museum where she had been an intern as a student. She started in the department of pre-schoolers but was moved around a lot. Her last job was in the office of the resource center. Although she had not elected to work primarily with special needs children, she was automatically given that group and felt that it was because she had a disability, though not a comparable one. Her main disappointment in the job, however, was that she felt patronized and not taken seriously. "I felt dismissed," she says. At the end of the year, she was not given the customary review of her work; after two years, she finally asked for one. Although her coworkers were very supportive, she felt the management could not deal with her disability.

After four years, Alicia decided to make a change and left to work for Partners for Youths with Disabilities, a nonprofit organization that matches adults with disabled children who have the same background, language, and often even the same disability. This was a good experience, Alicia noted. She served as an outreach specialist and was paired as a Big Sister to two girls who both had spina bifida. She met them about once a month. She has kept in touch with the two girls, one of whom lives in the same publicly subsidized building that she does in Somerville.

By 1993, Alicia says she felt burned out. She didn't like working in an office, going to the same place every day, and thinking about other people's problems. She wanted to do something different, so she decided to stop and think about her goals. She says, "I took a year off to get a fresh start." During that time, a friend who was at the Museum School in Boston suggested that she visit the school. "Art was what I always wanted to do," Alicia says, so when she visited her friend, she said to herself, "That's what I want," and arranged an interview for admissions. Even during her first interview, Alicia felt that the atmosphere and approach to her as a disabled person were both positive. She did not feel patronized and knew that if she was accepted, it would be based on her promise as an artist. The school asked her to come back with a portfolio. She spent a month getting her work together and after presenting it was accepted into the school.

Alicia has been at the Museum School for three years and expects she will take longer to complete the four-year program. She finds she is now goal-oriented and determined to succeed with her artwork. A review board gives her deadlines and goals for her work, but still allows her to adapt the program to her own pace. Several faculty members have served as her mentors. The presence of several other disabled students attests to the openness and inclusiveness of the school, she says. When I asked her about the kind of art she is presently interested in, she mentions Jackson Pollock and says she was initially a realist but now is more of an abstract expressionist. She also showed me a handsome ring that she wears, which is her own work.

Physically Alicia has to adapt her pace and accommodations. Her scooter provides her with mobility outside, and she uses her crutch inside. Her boyfriend gives her rides in a buggy attached to his bicycle and encourages her to practice meditation. She has had three surgeries connected with her cerebral palsy, but doesn't think they helped her much. She praises the Cerebral Palsy Association for helping those who need to get out into the community, but she has been fortunate in having her own friends and support group.

Alicia's attitude toward the able-bodied world is one of tolerance for people's mishandling of disability. She knows that some people just want to be helpful, but she often finds they make things worse. For instance, if they grab her arm it makes her become rigid, and sometimes, in attempting to help her across the street, they end up actually dragging her across. She is willing to adapt to the able-bodied world, but thinks the world must meet her halfway and that it definitely needs to make changes. She says we all have some kind of disabilities—whether physical or not—and we all need to find strength and believe in ourselves. Finally, Alicia insists that she doesn't need sympathy or doesn't want to be called courageous. She simply wants to be treated like another human being.

We discussed what Alicia thinks the disabled population needs most. She emphasizes the importance of education, believing that many disabled people do not get enough education and don't mature intellectually. "They don't grow up," she says, and "are like adolescents" who are not able to make good decisions about their future. They are channeled into jobs they don't like and can't get out of them. In her case, Alicia feels she did learn something from her jobs: she found out what she did not want to do. But she has felt pressure from the rehabilitation services to get back into the working world. She says they can't understand why she needs to take so long in her training, and they don't understand the work of an artist.

When I contacted Alicia for an update of our interview, she reported that she will graduate from the Museum School in 2003 and that she is living with her boyfriend of five years, who is also her personal care assistant. At the school she has concentrated on painting, drawing, and sculpting and describes her work as "mostly figurative."

Alicia sent me photocopies of two sculptures, which are part of her work. In one, a reclining figure looks toward the viewer, and in the other a child embraces an adult—perhaps a woman, though that is not clear from the photocopy. The sculptures give an impression of mass and strength, the figures seeming to grow out of the material. I was struck by the power and solidity of Alicia's sculptures, which contradict any weakness her impairments might suggest. Alicia feels she has found her own life work and is committed to trying to pursue it.

LAUREN

"I was a complete workaholic. All I did was my business."

or Lauren's interview, I drove to Marblehead on a beautiful
sunny day with my student assistant, Sarah, who asked if she
could come along. We found the house on a quiet suburban
street and were greeted hospitably at the front door by Lauren, a smiling, confident-looking young woman of thirty-six, in her wheelchair.
Despite a spinal cord injury six years previously, she was obviously
adept at maneuvering around her house and was at ease with being
interviewed about her life. Her husband also welcomed us and left us
as we settled in the living room to talk. Later he appeared with their
fourteen-month-old daughter, Diana, after her nap.

I asked Lauren to describe her accident, which occurred in 1995
while she was on vacation with a friend in Maine. They had brought
their bikes in Lauren's van, which she had bought for her flower shop
in Boston, and they had parked and started to walk their bikes over to
the ferry that was taking them to the island of Vinalhaven:

> While we were walking [the bikes] over to the ferry, I inadver-
> tently tripped on a rope, which was being used to mark where
> people [should] park their cars. [The rope] had worked itself into
> the sand so I did not notice it. I tripped on it. My bicycle went
> flying to the right and I went flying to the left. Unfortunately left
> was a sea wall and a thirteen-foot fall. So I landed thirteen feet
> later in a sitting position and I burst-fractured my lumbar one in
> my back. It was a beautiful sunny day in August and the sky was

blue, and you would never have thought that something like this was going to happen that day, but it did.

Lauren goes on to describe her immediate reaction even before the ambulance arrived and despite the extreme pain she felt. "A moment of clarity that I will never forget," she explains: "I pretty much came to a painful awareness that this was serious and that this was permanent and that not only was I not going to go for a bike ride that day, but that I might never bike ride again. And that I would be using a wheelchair for the rest of my life." At the same time, she says, "I understood what had happened to me and I knew what steps I needed to take, but I also knew that my life wasn't destroyed but that it had just been changed—dramatically."

She explains that she came to these immediate conclusions because of the image of two disabled people who came to her mind quite suddenly and unexpectedly. One was the journalist John Hockenberry, who had described his life as a correspondent in a wheelchair on National Public Radio. She recalls, "When I landed and my legs weren't working and they were numb, I told them to move and they would not move. I knew at that moment that I was just like John Hockenberry." The other was a student she knew at Northeastern University who had a spinal cord injury and used a wheelchair. "He was," she says, "an incredibly active, fit, very sociable man."

She continues, "I guess there [are] two role models right there that I probably never thought would have influenced me in any way, but they were the first two people I thought of when it happened. You know, they managed to date, they managed to go to college, they managed to have jobs—all that sort of stuff—so I think I am pretty fortunate to have known these two people in advance. By knowing them and seeing how full their lives were, the concept of disability wasn't as devastating to me, I think, as some people envision. A lot of people don't know people with disabilities before it happens to them."

Lauren lived a very active and varied life before her accident. After high school, where she was on the shot put and javelin team, she studied nursing for two years and then switched to study for a degree in sociology. She interrupted her college career to study at the American Floral Art School for a year in Chicago and finally decided to leave college, twelve credits short of a degree, to open a flower shop in Boston. She describes herself as a workaholic from the age of twelve, as a baby-sitter, and later, as a hostess working twenty hours a week during high school. She also worked nearly full-time all through college. When she owned her own flower shop, she worked sixty- to seventy-hour weeks, including weekends and late nights. She says, "I defined myself by my work. It came before friends, family, and social life. I never really made any money, but I always enjoyed working."

Not surprisingly, then, Lauren applied herself to her rehabilitation program with the same kind of energy she had given to her work. She says, "I had fantastic doctors," including a young orthopedic surgeon and neurologist at Maine Medical Center, where she was initially taken, as well as the doctors and therapists at New England Rehabilitation Hospital, where she spent two and a half months in intensive therapy. She credits her work in rehabilitation with giving her the techniques and preparation to return to an active life. She also fears that patients now are not getting the same level of care that she did:

When I was in [rehabilitation], I had a full day of therapy. They got me out of bed, and at nine o'clock in the morning I had my first physical therapy (PT) session, followed by my second PT session that went into an occupational therapy session. I had half an hour for lunch, then I was back in the PT room lifting weights again. They worked me six to seven hours a day. Those were the glory days of rehab, and I was part of the glory days. I think that now with budget cuts and insurance cuts, you get streamlined in and out of rehab before you even realize what happened to you.

Lauren noticed this trend of shorter treatment as a member of the National Spinal Cord Injury Association in her peer visits to women in rehab settings, and she worries about the consequences of these changes:

If this continues as a trend, disabled people, especially those with spinal cord injuries, are not going to get reassimilated into the community because they were left at the curb with only half the knowledge they needed. I think we are going to see less people going back to work. We are going to see a huge domino effect. People are not getting their drivers' licenses again. They aren't even finding out about hand controls for their cars. They're not learning what they need to do in order to function, to get back into life again. And what happens is they get stuck. They hit a wall. And at that wall is despair.

Whether Lauren benefited from "glory days" in her rehabilitation experience or whether her own energy and attitude were largely responsible for her success, she never despaired and was back at work full-time about eighteen months after the accident. She was released from New England Rehab Hospital on October 31, her wedding anniversary. During the following five months of outpatient rehab, she worked one day a week at the flower shop. Her husband was in the business with her, so he could continue to run it. She soon discovered that "my job was a very physical one":

> It hadn't really occurred to me that there's a lot of lifting of buckets, schlepping to the wholesale markets, and [handling] twenty-five-pound boxes of flowers. It wasn't that I was weak—I was certainly strong—but the dynamics of lifting those boxes from the floor to your lap! And buckets of water in a moving object tend to get water all over you! Reaching into my display cooler, which was about four feet deep, to get a lily for a customer was an athletic event. It was a lot more physical than I expected.

However, it was not her injury that made Lauren give up her shop. She was back at work full-time in May, and when she arrived at the shop that morning, she was welcomed by a bouquet of balloons from her husband. At lunchtime she received an eviction notice. They had accumulated about fifteen thousand dollars of debt while she was in rehab and could not meet the expensive rental payments on the shop. They renegotiated a payment plan and were fifteen hundred dollars short of paying off the debt when an accident damaged their van and once again wiped them out financially. When they failed to make the last payment on time, they were evicted officially. Although Lauren fought to save her business, calling her state senator, the mayor, and the media, she saw that she was forced to close. She says, "I made the decision not to keep fighting and not to reopen in another location. I had certainly given it the old college try by anyone's standards, but [I realized] it was time to move on."

Although giving up the flower shop was a very painful decision, Lauren feels in retrospect that it turned out well. For one thing, it freed her husband to find a job earning five times what they had been making collectively. For another, Lauren sold off her accounts to a shop in Copley Square and took a segment of her business—doing dried flowers and custom silk flowers for interior decorators—and used a friend's studio space for her work. After Lauren's daughter was born, she decided to work at home in a studio she and her husband built above the garage. Occasionally she does freelance work in a friend's flower shop, especially during holidays. Lauren explained that the many pots of flowers I had noticed on the porch off the kitchen were part of a fund-raiser she was preparing for Diana's day care center. "I think we are probably going to bring in about $750 worth of profit, she says. "OK for a first year."

As we talked, fourteen-month-old Diana appeared, carried by her father. She was a little shy and sleepy, but ran straight to her mother and got on her lap. After a few minutes when Lauren explained to Diana who we were, she called her husband to take the child and give her some juice, and asked him to keep her busy while we continued the interview.

The appearance of Diana introduced us to the story of her birth and of Lauren's pregnancy. I asked her to tell us about that experience. She says her accident put on hold the discussion she and her husband had begun about starting a family. In fact, she adds, while she was still in the hospital, she asked her husband if he thought he could stay in the marriage despite her changed condition. She says, "I fully expected him to leave, and we had a very frank talk in the rehab. I said, 'If you are going to leave, leave now, because I don't want to use you as a crutch to get over this. I want to get over it myself and not have to deal with a second trauma in my life later on.'" She adds, "He was crushed. He couldn't believe that I would ever think that about him."

About four years after the accident, Lauren says she had an overwhelming feeling that came to her in the middle of the night that she wanted to have a child. She says, "I turned to my husband and said, 'I'm ready.' And he goes, 'What for?' And I said, 'I'm ready to have kids. I've just got this inner burning desire to have a child and I don't know where it's come from, but I'm ready and want to go ahead with it.'"

Lauren had been told right from the day of her accident that the injury had not affected her reproductive organs in any way and that she could have children, although her pregnancy and the delivery might be difficult. She began to ask other women with spinal cord injuries how they managed their children. She asked specific questions such as, "How do you get the baby from the wheelchair into the car?" and "How do you get the baby out of the crib?" At first she was discouraged because they usually said their mother or husband helped them. That did not satisfy her because she wanted to feel that she could manage a baby by herself. So she began to borrow friends' children and attempted maneuvers from wheelchair to car and from crib to chair. With some practice and a lot of work, she succeeded. She says, "That was the important part. I *could* do it."

The next hurdle to overcome was to change or avoid the medication she took for spasticity because the medicine—Baclofen—can cause bone deformities in the developing fetus. Lauren demonstrated her condition by stomping her foot and showing us how it begins to shake. She explains that sometimes at night she gets extremely painful leg cramps, like a "charley horse," and her husband has to break up the cramp for her. To avoid the problem of the medication, she first used a metrical stimulation monitor to control the spasticity and was able to administer this treatment at home. She also did water therapy and was soon able to abandon the Baclofen. Soon afterward, she became pregnant. Not only did the spasticity slacken, but she finds that she has not had to return to the medication as long as she continues the regime of electrical stimulation and water therapy.

Characteristically, Lauren thoroughly prepared for her birthing. She showed us a two-page copy of patient information that she gave to her entire medical team. At the top of page one, after her name is the heading, "Read before Meeting with Patient." She then briefly but clinically describes her condition: "I have a Lumbar 1 incomplete spinal cord injury, with nearly full paralysis from the buttocks down in the back of the body and legs, and patchy sensation and use from the lower abdomen and down in the front." It continues the description and then admonishes, "Please do not compare me to the standard medical model." The rest of the document defines and describes such areas as bladder management, spasms, skin care, pain management, intravenous use and the role of the husband.

Despite these thorough instructions, she found that neither her doctor nor the hospital nurse had absorbed the significance of her condition and her lack of sensation in some areas. When she felt the pains of labor contractions in the middle of the night at five minutes apart, the doctor assured her she had plenty of time, though she reminded him of her record. By the time she got to the hospital the contractions were a minute and a half apart, but the nurse was in no hurry to get her to delivery, even though Lauren told her she felt the position of the baby had changed. Finally the nurse agreed to examine her and immediately hit the emergency button yelling, "Delivery team to [room] 114 stat!" The baby was delivered eight minutes later.

Lauren's description of her experience with the medical world at the birth of her child prompted her to comment, "That's what happens in a lot of medical situations. They are not familiar with your disability, and you end up having to give them a lesson, which is usually not well taken."

Lauren feels that her injury has actually made her a stronger, more focused person. She says, "I describe it to people as if the radio dial was turned to static and all of a sudden it tuned in. Suddenly it became very clear as to what was important and what wasn't important, and so as crazy and as zany as it sounds, I am pretty thankful for my injury." She concedes that other disabled people may not feel as lucky, and she tries to work with the National Spinal Cord Injury Association to help people get the information and education they need to gain independence. She says, "Living on a disability check is no life. It's subsistence. It's below the poverty level. The only hope for a disabled person is either to have a fund already or to go back to work because you can't live on what disability [insurance] pays."

She says that Massachusetts is a fairly good state to be disabled in because there are ways to continue to have medical insurance while working. She mentions Senator Edward Kennedy's so-called Back to Work bill, which allows people a certain period of time to maintain their medical benefits while trying to go back to work. She recalls that when her accident occurred, she and her husband had cut back expenses in the flower shop and had no health insurance. She was a Medicaid beneficiary for about eighteen months, and for her it was a source of "tremendous embarrassment." She says, "I never wanted to have to take some kind of public assistance." They are now covered by her husband's health benefits.

Lauren asked me why I did not use a wheelchair instead of crutches. She acknowledges that the common perception is that anyone would prefer to be upright. When people see her on her crutches, she says, they think she is getting better and say, "Oh, how well you're doing, Lauren. How terrific you look!" But she adds, "I feel a lot less disabled in my chair than I do upright. I am far more independent and quicker, and I can get ten times as much done in an hour in a wheelchair than I can on a set of crutches." She continues, "See, I hate going slow; I can't stand going slow. I can get across [the street] in a wheelchair faster than anyone can walk." Lauren uses a light sports wheelchair and says, "I am a huge advocate for the right durable medical equipment for the right person." We agree that a disabled person needs individualized medical equipment, but that is difficult to achieve. Often the equipment is not covered by insurance.

Lauren says the hardest thing that she confronts as a disabled person is "architecture," or accessibility. She explains, "If architecture could be made so that I can get around, I would have far less frustration every day. I've put out a number of freelance résumés and they're all in inaccessible shops. And I wonder if I'm not getting called back because of that." She continues, "What I need is very little, really. All I need is a hunk of plywood on a bunch of stacked buckets down at my level, and I need a thirty-two-inch clear path in order to get to the cooler or sink or the register. That doesn't even cost anybody anything as an accommodation. I'll climb the stairs if you take my wheelchair up, and I'll work for you by the day."

Lauren recalls one particular experience when she sent a résumé and called an employer to arrange an interview. When she arrived, she saw the terror on the man's face when he saw that she was in a wheelchair.

She says, "If you could have just had a camera. I knew by the look on his face that he would never hire me. He was terrified of me. He was speechless, stumbling over his words."

She has found some freelance jobs but, at times, customers are uncomfortable with being served by a disabled person. She describes a scene: "A customer comes in to buy a bouquet and I come right up to them and say, 'May I help you?' and they don't know what to say. You can tell they are quite uncomfortable about it. Frequently, I give them an option and say, 'Would you rather have Christine help you?' but that puts them in a really embarrassing position and so they reply, 'Oh no, no, no, that's fine. You can help me.' So then sometimes I try to reassure them by saying, 'I have eighteen years of experience in this' or 'All you need is the talent that's in my little fingers so I'm sure I can make just as nice a bouquet as everyone else here.'" Lauren concludes, "You just have to confront [the situation] with a little bit of charm and a little bit of humor and go right to the heart of the matter." We agreed that addressing her situation forthrightly has been her way of handling her life ever since her accident.

As we came to the end of our interview, Sarah asked Lauren if there has been anything that she wanted to do that she can't do since her accident. Her answer illustrates her attitude about her disability:

> There are only two things that I have been able to find that I can't do. I can't go hiking anymore and I can't get my sweaters off the top shelf. I have found the way to bike. I used to be an avid biker. I have a hand cycle out there in the garage. It's hand powered. I have done the Boston to New York AIDS ride twice. It's a 250-mile, three-day event. I never make it on the full course every day, but I put in a good 50 miles. And on arm power that's a lot! I can ski again by using the mono ski. I can dance again. My husband and I swing dance with the wheelchair and you wouldn't believe it. The wheelchair can be so fluid. I can just move to music the same way I did before. I still garden with a few little adaptive pieces of equipment like your basic Brookstone gardening knee stool, which gives me stability.

She concludes her list of successes by telling us about a solar-powered assist bicycle that is going to be demonstrated at a hand cycling event in Hadley. She plans to go and says, "I'm sure I am going to be suckered into buying another bike. Because that's something I have always loved."

Her plans for her future work are ambitious. She wants to make more money and expand her career. She feels confident that she can achieve those goals.

EPILOGUE

I started this project to learn about other disabled women and how they managed their lives. It has been a dynamic process, stretching over several years. I have been enlightened by much of disability literature and scholarship, but I have especially related to the stories of these women. After completing the thirty interviews and choosing eighteen of them to represent the themes and issues of the group, I wrote their stories using their transcripts. Finally, I contacted the eighteen women, sending them copies of their narratives. Some I have met with again. If they requested, I added additional comments or corrections they wished to make.

I am greatly enriched by what I have learned and shared. These women are strong and creative and determined. They are also often angry at society's lack of support and recognition of disabled people's potential talents and contributions. Many of them are engaged in trying to raise the consciousness of the "nondisabled" world. Their stories help us to redefine concepts and categories in our lives as women.

Since most of these women responded to my requests for interviews about work experience, they all had some acquaintance with the world of employment. I learned that success cannot be measured by the number of hours worked or by the earning power of these women. Although a number of them are self-supporting, the majority of the women interviewed are not. Nevertheless, they achieve, despite odds, self-sufficiency and self-determination, which I consider success. Some achieve this by receiving disability insurance and living in subsidized housing (about one-third of all those interviewed live in subsidized housing). These women work according to the capacity their disability allows, ranging from Debbie's four days a week as a social worker, to Elaine's half days as a hospital receptionist, to Louisa's full-time work as a lawyer. Judith sets her own time schedule in self-employment, and Kristen decided not to work while she was raising her daughter. As Judith says, "We need to expand our concept of work to take into consideration a person whose needs and abilities are not standard but who has assets and talents to offer."

It is clear that the chance of achievement in the world of work improves with education. Some of the women who work full-time have Ph.D.'s, law degrees, and M.A.'s, but educational advantages do not always guarantee work. As Kristen notes, being in a wheelchair can drastically lessen a person's opportunities of employment despite having a master's degree. Robin affirmed that even a Ph.D. and a successful career did not assure her of a position once she applied as a candidate with MS in a wheelchair. "People look at you funny in a wheelchair," she says.

Family support and resources have been factors in helping these women achieve self-sufficiency, but some had to assert their independence from family in order to achieve self-determination. Their stories reveal the complexity of the dependence/independence relationship and how it involves the role of the caretaker. Debbie spoke of needing to break away from the caretaking relationship with her mother, but her brother, writing his commentary after her death, noted how much her family had sought to give her that independence.

Although these women's life stories have revealed the relevance of family support and resources, education, societal accommodations, and the severity and onset of their disabilities, the outcome to the challenges they face is the result of a confluence of these factors. Their stories defy broad conclusions and illustrate particular negotiations by these women between their impairments and their environment.

I learned that the kind of success these women have achieved has largely been due to the way they have been able to claim their disabilities and confront the challenge of living in a nondisabled world. All of them agree that disability is not just a medical condition with or without a cure. They see disability as a socially constructed category that creates public discrimination, personal dismissal, and stereotyping. But they do not see themselves as victims. Their stories reveal moments and turning points when they recognize that, for better or worse, their disabilities are part of themselves just as race or gender or class is.

Although these women share many common experiences, their stories are unique as well. For instance, they show different ways of describing their disability and their relationship to it. Attitudes range from perceiving a disability as an "inconvenience" and not necessarily a liability, to feeling "broken" by it, to seeing it as something to test one's will and strength. For instance, Adrienne insisted that her disability of blindness is just something she has to factor in her life "the way that someone with a two-hour commute to work does." It's just a fact, she said. Debbie, despite severe physical impairments from cerebral palsy and dependence on personal care assistants, insisted that her disability is not "who I am. It's something I happen to have."

Neither Robin nor Carol, however, would characterize their disabilities as an "inconvenience." Robin argued that a progressive disability is particularly difficult because she does not know what to expect and has no guidelines or road map to deal with what is coming. She spoke of the rapid transformations of her body in one year from multiple sclerosis. She lost thirteen pounds and is no longer able to walk or to write by hand. Carol described the multiple disabilities she experienced after her accident. Because her impairments are largely invisible, she had to fight for support and accommodations even as she lost her job, her home, and her close relationships.

Doris's progressive disability of muscular dystrophy made her search for a spiritual context for her condition. She described relating her feelings of helplessness and brokenness to a revelation when she saw Christ on the cross as representing the immobility and vulnerability of a paraplegic. She found that this image gave her a way of connecting her disability to her faith. In another context, Judith described her gradual understanding of her multiple chemical sensitivities as part of the human relationship of mind and body.

Like several other women, Lauren emphasized individual willpower and determination in her relationship to her disability. Even at the scene of her catastrophic accident, which resulted in a spinal cord injury, she began to assess the extent of her injuries as she waited for the ambulance. She determined that although she would probably be using a wheelchair for the rest of her life, her life would be dramatically changed but not destroyed. She insists that her disability has actually had a positive affect on her as a person. Although she places the responsibility for returning to an active life largely on the disabled person, she argues that the nondisabled world must also take responsibility in providing a supportive environment for disabled people.

All these women shared a common awareness at some point in their lives that they lived in two worlds—the world they knew as a disabled person and the world of the nondisabled. They all had to confront discrimination and marginalization from society. Most of the women felt they had been more discriminated against or stereotyped for their disability than for their gender, and one of them felt even more than from race.

At the same time, they often identified a gendered cultural attitude and described the double discrimination, or "layered" discrimination,"[1] of being a woman and disabled. Several women felt infantilized by potential employers. As Adrienne said about the demeaning attitude she experienced in interviews, which she called patriarchal, "You could be a cute little child if you had a disability, but you couldn't be a full-grown adult." Others found paternalism in their workplace. Sally spoke of an "old boy network" and described a corporate culture of discrimination toward women. She felt that women didn't understand how important it was to be assertive, particularly if they were disabled. She concluded, "You really have to do more than anybody else would do."

Barbara felt that the gender discrimination she experienced as a biochemist in graduate school and later at work was worse than the discrimination she encountered as a disabled person. She also described her mother's low expectations for her achievement because of her disability as well as her gender. Her mother, she said, felt she would never earn a living and that "I would surely never get married." This prejudice worked another way in the world of little people, according to June. Dwarfism, she said, is more likely to affect men's marital chances than women's. More females marry into the "normal" world than males, due, she thought, to the macho image of height and strength that men encounter in society.

One of the women I interviewed, who had polio and who had recovered from alcohol and drug addiction, described male oppression in her life. After experiencing domestic violence from her father and low expectations from her mother while growing up, she found herself repeatedly with abusive male partners. Looking back, she characterized her low self-esteem, which prevented her from breaking out of bad relationships: "I guess," she said, "I felt that was all I could expect." She works now as a volunteer in a battered women's shelter and hopes to get a degree in counseling so that she can help other abused women. Although her experience of sexual abuse was not common in this particular group of women interviewed, it is a serious issue among disabled women.[2]

A number of women felt that they had been channeled during high school or rehabilitation counseling into traditionally female job tracks with little encouragement to explore options or form ambitious goals. Alicia was guided into work with disabled children but found that the work was not her calling. She took a year off to reflect on her future and decided to study art.

Although motherhood was not a major focus of the interviews, many of the women discussed their experiences as mothers or, sometimes, their concern about whether they would have the chance to be mothers. Of the twelve women who were married, ten of them had children and one adopted a child as a single parent. All of them acknowledged that their disability, no matter at what stage it had developed in their lives, had impacted their role as mothers but had not changed their confidence in that role. Society did not always show the same confidence in them. Doris, who had five children—"that's what Catholic girls did in those days"—said she remembered that at her wedding her aunt, noticing her difficulty in getting up the church steps, remarked, "How is that child ever going to be [able to be] pregnant?" Lauren, twenty years later, planned her pregnancy and birthing with the same kind of care and resolve that she showed in rehabilitation from her spinal cord injury. However, her medical team all but ignored the careful technical instructions she had prepared about her needs and condition. Fortunately, she gave birth to a healthy baby daughter and proved that it could be done.

The question of children's reactions to their disabled mothers, a subject worthy of another study, came up occasionally and revealed very different experiences. Kristen felt that her daughter and her daughter's friends had taken her disability in stride. Judith acknowledged that during the worst periods of her depression and hospitalization, her relationship with her daughter had been strained and that "she experienced the other side of a lot of what I've been through." Even now, she says, she "keeps her distance." Louisa, however, felt that although her aneurysm and the subsequent trauma were hard on her children, particularly her daughter, who was fifteen at the time, it also fostered a growth experience for them both.

One woman, who is deaf, describes a different relationship with her children. She felt that her disability had a tremendous influence on them and found it hard to believe that my children—when she asked me about them—did not feel anger or resentment at growing up with a disabled person. She explained that her son and daughter did not feel safe with her as a single deaf parent. She could not answer the phone or monitor their life, and they often had to interpret for her in the hearing world. She recalled that when her son was four years old, he told a grocery store clerk "My mother is deaf. I'll speak for her." Clearly the relationship between disability and mothering is complex and varied for these women, and a subject only touched upon in our interviews.

Although the stories of these women have many differences, they also agree on what practical and cultural changes need to be made to give disabled people, and women in particular, a chance to participate fully in society. Their major areas of agreement are summarized next.

All agreed that the medical world needs to change its attitude toward disability. Some transformations have occurred, but much more needs to be done. The work that Elaine and others are doing with medical students is vital in getting medical personnel to listen to their patients, who, after all, know their bodies best and can tell doctors how they function. Alice echoed this advice and added that doctors must become knowledgeable about specific disabilities and the effects they have on their medical specialties. She learned, for instance, that her gynecologist did not connect her spasticity with endometriosis. Robin called for better rehabilitation and guidelines for those with progressive diseases such as multiple sclerosis.

Many women pointed out that health professionals, such as therapists, counselors, and educators, are still too often using the medical model for disability. They need to understand the changes that have come about as a result of the disability movement. The women spoke of the need for improvement, especially in the way women are advised and often discouraged from pursuing nontraditional careers and life choices.

No matter what the disability, but particularly for the physically disabled, the women agreed that overwhelming physical barriers and lack of accommodations in the environment prevent the disabled from being contributing members of society. Kristen pointed out that lowering cash registers would open up jobs for people in wheelchairs. Robin described the extraordinary amount of time she had to spend traveling in her wheelchair a short distance to her doctor because of the lack of curb cuts. She also described the difficulty in finding accessible housing. Even Lauren, as positive as she was about her ability to do everything, cited "architecture" as the main barrier to her success in returning to the florist business. Several women described the blatant lack of accommodations in institutions or corporations, which forced them finally to initiate lawsuits. Barbara and Virginia both work to educate institutions and society about universal design and other concepts of bringing equity to the disabled, but they both agree it is a difficult battle. All agreed that the ADA needs implementation.

Finally, all agreed that cultural attitudes and norms need to change. A redefinition of terms such as "normal"—rejecting the normal/abnormal dichotomy—and a new understanding of the category of disability are needed. Feminists and theorists, such as Rosemarie Garland-Thomson, Barbara Hillyer, and Susan Wendell, have begun to look at these terms and issues, particularly as they affect women. They argue that issues of disabled women are issues for all society. Just as we find that the changes recommended by universal design actually help and accommodate everyone, we shall also find that changes in cultural attitudes will help us toward a more just society.

My own attitude and understanding of disability has changed as a result of this project. At one time, growing up and as a young woman, I tried to ignore my disability and the disabled community and concentrated on overachieving. When I began to accept my own body and impairments as part of who I was, I became aware that I was indeed part of the disabled community. Now, listening to other disabled women and participating in the disability movement, I know that we are all part of the human community and share a commonalty, which is a spectrum of different characteristics and abilities. A cultural transformation is needed for all of us to understand this.

Lennard Davis has addressed this need of transformation in our thinking. In *Bending Over Backwards: Disability, Dismodernism, and Other Difficult Positions*, he examines the category of disability and how it relates to his newly invented concept of "dismodernism." He writes, "Dismodernism argues for a commonalty of bodies within the notion of difference. It is too easy to say, 'We're all disabled.' But it is possible to say that we are all disabled by injustice and oppression of various kinds. We are all nonstandard, and it is under that standard that we should be able to found the Dismodernist ethic."[3]

NOTES

Introduction

1. U.S. Census Bureau, "2000 Population Survey," http://www.pcensus.com.
2. L. Jans and S. Stoddard, *Chartbook on Women and Disability in the United States, 1999* (Washington D.C.: U.S. Department of Education, National Institute on Disability and Rehabilitation Research), 23.
3. U.S. Census Bureau, "2000 Population Survey."
4. U.S. Department of Labor, "Women with Disabilities: Facts on Working Women," *Women's Bureau* 92, no. 2 (March 1992): 3.
5. Sally A. Fulton and Edward J. Sabornie, "Evidence of Employment Inequality among Females with Disabilities," *Journal of Special Education* 28, no. 2 (1994): 162.
6. Adrienne Asch and Michelle Fine, "Nurturance, Sexuality, and Women with Disabilities," in *The Disability Studies Reader*, ed. Lennard J. Davis (New York: Routledge, 1997), 241.
7. Rosemarie Garland-Thomson, *Extraordinary Bodies: Figuring Physical Disability in American Culture and Literature* (New York: Columbia University Press, 1997), 46.
8. H. Stephen Kaye, "Is the Status of People with Disabilities Improving?" *Disability Statistics Abstract* no. 21 (May 1998): 2–3.
9. Garland-Thomson, *Extraordinary Bodies*, 29.
10. Nancy Mairs, *Waist High in the World: A Life among the Nondisabled* (Boston: Beacon Press,1996), 51.
11. Carol J. Gill, "Four Types of Integration in Disability Identity Development," *Journal of Vocational Rehabilitation* 9 (1997): 43.
12. Mairs, *Waist High in the World*, 83.
13. Asch and Fine, "Nurturance, Sexuality, and Women with Disabilities," 247.
14. Rosemarie Garland-Thomson, "Integrating Disability, Transforming Feminist Theory," *NWSA Journal: Feminist Disability Studies* 14, no. 3 (fall 2002): 6.
15. Cynthia Anne Tighe, "Working at Disability: A Qualitative Study of the Meaning of Health and Disability for Women with Physical Disabilities," *Disability and Society* 18, no. 4 (2001): 524.
16. Carol Woodhams, "Disability in the Workplace: Hidden Disabilities and Human Resources Practice," *Disability Studies Quarterly* 20, no. 3 (summer 2000): 276.
17. Gill, "Four Types of Integration," 45.
18. Irving Goffman, *Stigma: Notes on the Management of Spoiled Identity* (Englewood Cliffs, N.J.: Prentice-Hall, 1963), 74.

19. U.S. Department of Labor, "Women with Disabilities," 3.
20. Ibid., 3.
21. Doris Zames Fleischer and Frieda Zames, *The Disability Rights Movement: From Charity to Confrontation* (Philadelphia: Temple University Press, 2001),13.
22. Ibid., 39.
23. Jenny Morris, ed., introduction to *Encounters with Strangers: Feminism and Disability* (London: Women's Press, 1996),14–15.
24. Jenny Morris, "Impairment and Disability: Constructing an Ethics of Care That Promotes Human Rights," *Hypatia: A Journal of Feminist Philosophy* 16, no. 4 (fall 2001): 10. Morris makes a distinction between *impairment* ("a characteristic, feature or attribute within an individual which is long term and may or may not be the result of a disease or injury") and *disability* ("the disadvantage or restriction of activity caused by society which takes little or no account of people who have impairments"), 2. I do not make this distinction in this work.

PART 1 THE WAY WE SEE OURSELVES

1. Thomas G. Couser, *Recovering Bodies: Illness, Disability, and Life Writing* (Madison: University of Wisconsin Press, 1997), 13.
2. Gill, "Four Types of Integration." 13.
3. Paul K. Longmore and Lauri Umansky, eds., *The New Disability History: American Perspectives* (New York: New York University Press, 2001), 20.
4. Garland-Thomson, *Extraordinary Bodies*, 6.
5. Barbara Hillyer, *Feminism and Disability* (Norman: University of Oklahoma Press, 1993), 216.
6. Ibid., 216.
7. Gill, "Four Types of Integration," 44.
8. Marsha Saxton and Florence Howe, eds., *With Wings: An Anthology of Literature by and about Women with Disabilities* (New York: Feminist Press, 1987), 76.
9. Ibid., 77.

PART 2 THE WAY THE WORLD SEES US

1. Nora Ellen Groce, *Everyone Here Spoke Sign Language: Hereditary Deafness on Martha's Vineyard* (Cambridge: Harvard University Press, 1985), 50.
2. Ibid., 5.
3. Ibid., 108.
4. Garland-Thomson, *Extraordinary Bodies*, 43.
5. Harlan Lane, "Construction of Deafness," in *The Disability Studies Reader*, ed. Lennard J. Davis (New York: Routledge, 1997). Lane writes that two constructions of deafness compete in shaping deaf people's destinies: "The one construes deaf as a category of disability, the other construes deaf as designating a linguistic minority" (154).
6. Kenny Fries, introduction to *Staring Back: The Disability Experience from the Inside Out* (New York: Plume, 1997), 1.

7. Zames Fleischer and Zames, *The Disability Rights Movement*, 28.
8. Ibid., 28.

PART 3 THE WAY WE WORK

1. Marta Russell, "Russell's Index," in *Beyond Ramps: Disability at the End of the Social Contract* (Monroe, Maine: Common Courage Press, 1998).
2. Mary Johnson, "Disabling a Civil Right," *The Nation*, February 11, 2002, 23.
3. Ibid., 22.
4. Russell, "Russell's Index," 82. Russell argues that "it is a discrimination to deny a disabled person who can work an opportunity to do so, but it is not 'special' treatment for people who cannot work to be guaranteed a humane standard of living—rather it is a measure of a just civilization that they are decently provided for" (82).
5. Massachusetts Rehabilitation Commission, *SSDI and the Decision to Return to Work: A Study* (Boston: Office of Consumer Involvement), September 1997.

EPILOGUE

1. Alessandra Iantaffi, "Women and Disability in Higher Education," in *Breaking Boundaries: Women in Higher Education*, ed. Louise Morley and Val Walsh (London: Taylor and Francis, 1996), 80. Iantaffi writes, "I define this type of oppression [experienced by women] as 'layered' rather than as a 'double' disadvantage because the discriminations disabled women experience operate 'simultaneously'" (180).
2. Asch and Fine, "Nurturance, Sexuality, and Women with Disabilities," 249.
3. Lennard J. Davis, *Bending Over Backwards: Disability, Dismodernism, and Other Difficult Positions* (New York: New York University Press, 2002), 31–32.

GLOSSARY

Alzheimer's disease (AD) A neurodegenerative disorder mainly characterized by the progressive and irreversible loss of nerve cells (neurons) located in specific brain areas: the hippocampus and the polymodal association areas. AD is a disease that attacks the brain and results in impaired memory, thinking, and behavior. It is the most common form of dementia.

American Association for the Advancement of Science (AAAS) Publisher of *Science*, the AAAS is the world's largest general scientific society.

Americans with Disabilities Act of 1990 (ADA) The civil rights guarantee for persons with disabilities in the United States. It provides protection from discrimination for individuals on the basis of disability. The ADA extends civil rights protections for people with disabilities to employment in the public and private sectors, transportation, public accommodations, services provided by state and local government, and telecommunication relay services.

Aneurysm An abnormal blood-filled dilatation of a blood vessel and especially an artery resulting from disease of the vessel wall.

Bioethics A discipline dealing with the ethical implications of biological research and applications, especially in medicine.

Braille Invented by Frenchman Louis Braille (1809–1852), Braille is a system of writing for the blind that uses characters made up of raised dots. By age fifteen, Louis had developed the system that we know today as Braille, which employs a six-dot cell and is based on normal spelling. He also went on to lay the foundation for the Braille representation of music.

Cerebral palsy (CP) A motor disorder caused by damage to the central nervous system before or during birth. Sometimes associated with a lack of oxygen, it has been described as a "bruise on the brain." Main symptoms include a general weakness, lack of limb and muscle coordination, impaired sensory perception, and sometimes impaired intelligence.

Chapter 766 A law passed by all state legislatures that requires all school systems to provide special needs programs for students. The programs provide specialized services to assist students in getting the full benefit from their educational opportunity. The degree of assistance, as well as the type of assistance, varies according to students' needs.

Committee on Equal Opportunities in Science and Engineering (CEOSE) A congressionally mandated advisory committee to the National Science Foundation.

Crohn's disease A chronic inflammatory disease of the intestines. It primarily causes ulcerations in the small and large intestines, but can affect the digestive system anywhere between the mouth and the anus.

Endometriosis A disease in which abnormal tissue grows in the abdomen and other places in the body. It causes internal bleeding, inflammation, scarring, severe pain and fatigue, and sometimes infertility. It is similar to cancer, but it is not cancer, and it is almost never fatal. It can be treated with pain medication, hormones, and surgery.

Equal Employment Opportunity Commission (EEOC) The EEOC works to make sure that workplaces are free from all forms of unlawful discrimination and harassment, and provides programs to assist members of EEOC groups to overcome past or present disadvantage. This means having workplace rules, policies, practices, and behaviors that are fair and do not disadvantage people because they belong to particular groups.

Gallaudet University Formerly Gallaudet College, it was founded in 1864 and is the only liberal arts university in the world designed exclusively for deaf and hard of hearing students. Communication among faculty, staff, and students, whether in or out of the classroom, is through the use of both sign language and written and spoken English.

Helen Keller (1880–1968) An American author and educator who was blind and deaf. Keller graduated with a bachelor of arts degree cum laude at Radcliffe College. Her most famous work is *The Story of My Life*.

Medicaid A jointly funded federal-state health insurance program for certain low-income and needy people. It covers approximately thirty-six million individuals including children, the elderly, the disabled, and people who are eligible to receive federally assisted income maintenance payments.

Multiple sclerosis (MS) A demyelinating disease marked by patches of hardened tissue in the brain or the spinal cord. It randomly attacks the central nervous system, wearing away bodily control. Symptoms may range from numbness to paralysis and blindness. The progress, severity, and specific symptoms cannot be foreseen. Most people are diagnosed with MS between the ages of twenty and forty.

Muscular dystrophy (MD) The name for a group of inherited disorders in which strength and muscle bulk gradually decline. Nine types of muscular dystrophies are generally recognized, all of which are marked by muscle weakness as the major symptom. The distribution of symptoms, age of onset, and progression differ significantly. No cure is available for any of the muscular dystrophies, but many treatments can overcome specific problems associated with these conditions.

National Association of the Deaf (NAD) Established in 1880, NAD is the oldest and largest constituency organization safeguarding the accessibility and civil rights of twenty-eight million deaf and hard of hearing Americans in education, employment, health care, and telecommunications.

National Institutes of Health (NIH) The steward of medical and behavioral research for the nation. Its mission is science in pursuit of fundamental knowledge about the nature and behavior of living systems and the application of that knowledge to extend healthy life and reduce the burdens of illness and disability.

New York City Commission on Human Rights The commission's human rights law is one of the most comprehensive civil rights laws in the nation. The law prohibits discrimination in employment, housing, and public accommodations based on race, color, creed, age, national origin, alienage or citizenship status, gender (including gender identity and sexual harassment), sexual orientation, disability, or marital status.

Oralism The advocacy or use of the oral method of teaching the deaf. A technique used with deaf children in which the use of sign language such as ASL is discouraged and lipreading is emphasized.

Osteogenesis imperfecta (OI) A group of genetic diseases of collagen in which the bones are formed improperly, making them fragile and prone to breaking. It occurs in about one of every twenty thousand births. No treatments are available to cure OI, nor are most of its complications preventable. Most treatments are aimed at treating the fractures and bone deformities caused by OI.

Poliomyelitis An acute infectious disease caused by the poliovirus and characterized by fever, motor paralysis, and atrophy of skeletal muscles often with permanent disability and deformity and marked by inflammation of nerve cells in the anterior gray matter in each lateral half of the spinal cord.

Post-polio syndrome (PPS) A condition that affects polio survivors anywhere from ten to forty years after recovery from an initial paralytic attack. PPS is characterized by a further weakening of muscles that were previously affected by the polio infection.

Quadriplegic A person who is permanently unable to move any of his or her arms or legs, often because the spine has been injured.

Rehabilitation Act of 1973 A law that prohibits discrimination on the basis of disability in local programs and activities benefiting from federal financial assistance; its enforcement has resulted in improved program accessibility for disabled persons in health care, social services, recreation, housing, transportation, and so on. Section 504 of the Rehabilitation Act of 1973 states: "No otherwise qualified handicapped individual in the United States . . . shall, solely by reason of . . . handicap, be excluded from participation in, be denied the benefits of, or be subjected to discrimination under any program or activity receiving federal financial assistance."

Social security disability insurance (SSDI)   Insurance that pays benefits to disabled people and certain members of their families if they are "insured," meaning that they worked long enough and paid social security taxes.

Spasticity   The condition of certain muscles being in a constant state of muscle contraction. Spasticity causes normally movable parts to become rigid and have exaggerated tendon reflexes.

Spina bifida   A condition, varying in severity, that develops in a fetus early in pregnancy. It occurs when the bones (vertebrae) that make up a baby's spine do not form properly, allowing the spinal cord to bulge out of the spine.

Spinal fusion   A "welding" process by which two or more of the small bones (vertebrae) that make up the spinal column are fused together with bone grafts and internal devices such as metal rods to heal into a single, solid bone.

Supplemental security income (SSI)   The Social Security Administration (SSA) administers this program. The SSA pays monthly benefits to people with limited income and resources who are age sixty-five or older, blind, or disabled. Blind or disabled children, as well as adults, can get SSI. Under SSI, a child is defined as being under age eighteen, or under age twenty-two and in school or other training to prepare for a job, and unmarried.

Systemic lupus (also called SLE)   A chronic inflammatory condition caused by an autoimmune disease. It may cause skin rashes, arthritis, anemia, seizures, or psychiatric illness, and often affects internal organs including the kidneys, lungs, and heart. Once a disease with high mortality, SLE is now considered a chronic disease.

Tai chi   Tai chi, as it is practiced in the West today, can perhaps best be thought of as a moving form of yoga and meditation combined. It is primarily practiced for its health benefits.

TMJ   Temporomandibular joint, or the jaw joint. The TMJs are the small joints in front of each ear that attach the lower jaw (mandible) to the skull.

TMJ diseases/disorders   A complex and poorly understood set of conditions, manifested by pain in the area of the jaw and associated muscles and limitations in the ability to make the normal movements of speech, facial expression, eating, chewing, and swallowing.

Transverse myelitis   A neurological disorder caused by inflammation across both sides of one level, or segment, of the spinal cord. Attacks of inflammation can damage or destroy myelin, the fatty insulating substance that covers nerve cell fibers. This damage causes nervous system scars that interrupt communications between the nerves in the spinal cord and the rest of the body.

SUGGESTED READINGS

Asch, Adrienne, and Michelle Fine. "Nurturance, Sexuality, and Women with Disabilities." In *The Disability Studies Reader*, ed. Lennard J. Davis. New York: Routledge, 1997.

Asch, Adrienne, and Erik Parens, eds. *Prenatal Testing and Disability Rights*. Washington, D.C.: Georgetown University Press, 2000.

Brooks, Nancy A., and Mary Jo Deegan, eds. *Women and Disability: The Double Handicap*. New Brunswick, N.J.: Transaction Books, 1985.

Browne, Susan E., Debra Coners, and Nanci Stem, eds. *With the Power of Each Breath: A Disabled Women's Anthology*. Pittsburgh: Cleis Press, 1985.

Brueggemann, Brenda. *Lend Me Your Ears*. Washington D.C.: Gallaudet University Press, 1999.

Campling, Jo, ed. *Images of Ourselves: Disabled Women Talking*. Boston: Routledge and Kegan Paul, 1981.

Couser, Thomas G. *Recovering Bodies: Illness, Disability, and Life Writing*. Madison: University of Wisconsin Press,1997.

Davis, Lennard J. *Bending Over Backwards: Disability, Dismodernism, and Other Difficult Positions*. New York: New York University Press, 2002.

——, ed. *The Disability Studies Reader*. New York: Routledge, 1997.

Fine, Michelle, and Adrienne Asch., eds. *Women with Disabilities: Essays in Psychology, Policy, and Politics*. Philadelphia: Temple University Press, 1988.

Finger, Anne. *Past Due: A Story of Disability, Pregnancy, and Birth*. Seattle: Seal Press, 1990.

Frank, Arthur W. *The Wounded Storyteller: Body, Illness, and Ethics*. Chicago: University of Chicago Press, 1995.

Garland-Thomson, Rosemarie. *Extraordinary Bodies: Figuring Physical Disability in American Culture and Literature*. New York: Columbia University Press, 1997.

——. "Integrating Disability, Transforming Feminist Theory." *NWSA Journal: Feminist Disability Studies* 14, no. 3 (fall 2002): 1–32.

Goffman, Irving. *Stigma: Notes on the Management of Spoiled Identity*. Englewood Cliffs, N.J.: Prentice-Hall, 1963.

Groce, Nora Ellen. *Everyone Here Spoke Sign Language*. Cambridge: Harvard University Press, 1985.

Hans, Asha, and Annie Patri, eds. *Women, Disability, and Identity*. New Delhi, India: Sage Publications, 2003.

Hillyer, Barbara. *Feminism and Disability*. Norman: University of Oklahoma Press, 1993.

Hockenberry, John. *Moving Violations: War Zones, Wheelchairs, and Declarations of Independence*. New York: Hyperion, 1995.

Keith, Lois, ed. *What Happened to You? Writing by Disabled Women*. New York: New Press, 1996.

Kleege, Georgina. *Sight Unseen*. New Haven, Conn.: Yale University Press, 1999.

Linton, Simi. *Claiming Disability: Knowledge and Identity*. New York: New York University Press, 1998.

Longmore, Paul K., and Lauri Umansky, eds. *The New Disability History: American Perspectives*. New York: New York University Press, 2001.

Lonsdale, Susan. *Women and Disability: The Experience of Physical Disability among Women*. Durham, N,C.: Duke University Press, 1996.

Mairs, Nancy. *Waist High in the World: A Life among the Nondisabled*. Boston: Beacon Press, 1996.

Matthews, Gwyneth Ferguson. *Voices from the Shadows: Women with Disabilities Speak Out*. Toronto: Women's Press, 1993.

Mitchell, David, and Sharon Snyder, eds. *The Body and Physical Difference: Discourses of Disability*. Ann Arbor: University of Michigan Press, 1997.

———. *Narrative Prosthesis: Disability and the Dependencies of Discourse*. Ann Arbor: University of Michigan Press, 2000.

Morris, Jenny, ed. *Encounters with Strangers: Feminism and Disability*. London: Women's Press, 1996.

———. "Impairment and Disability: Constructing an Ethics of Care That Promotes Human Rights." *Hypatia: A Journal of Feminist Philosophy* 16, no. 4 (fall 2001): 10.

Panzarino, Conni. *The Me in the Mirror*. Seattle: Seal Press, 1994.

Poole, Judith. *More than Meets the Eye: Energy*. Watertown, Maine: Pooled Resources, 1999.

Rousso, Harilyn. *Disabled, Female, and Proud! Stories of Ten Women with Disabilities*. Boston: Exceptional Parent Press, 1988.

Russell, Marta. *Beyond Ramps: Disability at the End of the Social Contract*. Monroe, Maine: Common Courage Press, 1998.

Saxton, Marsha, and Florence Howe, eds. *With Wings: An Anthology of Literature by and about Women with Disabilities*. New York: Feminist Press, 1987.

Snyder, Sharon L., Jo Bruggemann, and Rosemarie Garland-Thomson, eds. *Disability Studies: Enabling the Humanities*. New York: Modern Language Association of America, 2002.

Wendell, Susan. *The Rejected Body: Feminist Philosophical Reflections on Disability*. New York: Routledge, 1996.

———. "Towards a Feminist Theory of Disability." In *The Disability Studies Reader*, ed. Lennard J. Davis. New York: Routledge, 1997.

Wilson, James C., and Cynthia Lewiecki-Wilson, eds. *Embodied Rhetorics: Disability in Language and Culture*. Carbondale: Southern Illinois University Press, 2001.

Women and Disability: The Double Handicap. Special issue of the *Journal of Sociology and Social Welfare* 8, no. 2 (1981).

Zames Fleischer, Doris, and Frieda Zames. *The Disability Rights Movement: From Charity to Confrontation.* Philadelphia: Temple University Press, 2001.

Zola, Irving. *Missing Pieces: A Chronicle of Living with a Disability.* Philadelphia: Temple University Press, 1982.

DATE DUE

GAYLORD | No. 2333 | | PRINTED IN U.S.A.